Fifty Years, Fifty Stories

THE MENNONITE MISSION IN SOMALIA, 1953-2003

To all who work for peace in Somalia

Published in association with
Eastern Mennonite Missions, Salunga, Pennsylvania

Fifty Years, Fifty Stories

THE MENNONITE MISSION IN SOMALIA, 1953-2003

Omar Eby

Foreword by John A. Lapp

DreamSeeker Books
TELFORD, PENNSYLVANIA
an imprint of
Cascadia Publishing House

Copublished with
Herald Press
Scottdale, Pennsylvania

Cascadia Publishing House orders, information, reprint permissions:
contact@CascadiaPublishingHouse.com
1-215-723-9125
126 Klingerman Road, Telford PA 18969
www.CascadiaPublishingHouse.com

Fifty Years, Fifty Stories
Copyright © 2003 by Cascadia Publishing House,
Telford, PA 18969
All rights reserved.
DreamSeeker Books is an imprint of
Cascadia Publishing House
Copublished with Herald Press, Scottdale, PA
Library of Congress Catalog Number: 2003041035
ISBN: 1-931038-17-1
Printed in the United States of America by Versa Press
Book and cover design by Greg Yoder

The paper used in this publication is recycled and meets the
minimum requirements of American National Standard for Information Sciences—
Permanence of Paper for Printed Library Materials, ANSI Z39.48-1984.

Library of Congress Cataloguing-in-Publication Data
Eby, Omar, 1935-
    Fifty Years, Fifty Stories : the Mennonite mission in Somalia, 1953-2003 / Omar Eby ;
foreword by John A. Lapp
        p. cm.
"Published in association with Eastern Mennonite Missions, Salunga, Pennsylvania."
ISBN 1-931038-17-1 (alk. paper)
    1. Mennonites--Missions--Somalia--History--20th century. 2. Missions--Somalia--
History--20th century. 3. Somalia--Church history--20th century. 4. Mennonites--So-
malia--History--20th century. 5. Missionaries--Somalia--History--20th century. 6. Mis-
sionaries--United States--History--20th century. I. Title.

BV3625.S56E29 2003
266'.976773--dc21
                                                                                    2003041035

          12 11 10 09 08 07 06 05 04 03   10 9 8 7 6 5 4 3 2 1

Contents

Foreword

The heart and soul of Christian mission is "bearing witness." The Gospel of John (KJV) uses this classic phrase for the divine task assigned to John the Baptist, the Holy Spirit, and the disciples of Jesus. Before anyone can be invited to faith, before any church can be established, followers of Jesus the Christ "bear witness" to the "one light" coming into the world.

Decades before the recent interest in the Islamic world, Eastern Mennonite Missions felt called to work in Somalia. Other churches have worked in this almost totally Islamic environment. None would be considered very successful. Yet, this inspiring piece of mission literature describes well the passion to "bear witness" amid a well-established traditional society.

The story of the church's witness is always embedded in a larger context. In Somalia, this context is as intense as the hot desert winds. Situated on the Horn of Africa across the Gulf of Aden from the Arabian peninsula, Somalia can be viewed as a part of the Islamic heartland. In 1953 Somalia was still an Italian and British protectorate. Like a dozen other African states, Somalia became independent in 1960. But the promise of a brighter future soon foundered on the inherent conflicts of clan-dominated politics. The pressure for a unitary society forced the mission to cease its work in 1976. Mennonites returned in 1980—only to be forced to flee again amid civil war in 1991. Nonetheless, the work continues.

Although only an interval in the history of the Christian church, this small mission touched all the major questions of contemporary missionary style and strategy. How should the gospel be expressed in a restrictive setting? What does it mean to respect the host people and their culture? Does this respect extend to another religion? How do outsiders relate to local conflicts? How much personal risk should missional people take? When does the stranger become more of a liability than a helper in a conflictual situation? Can a church representing the peace tradition serve as an alternative to the Christian crusading tradition? How does the contemporary church respond to modern day Nicodemuses? Must "bearing witness" always lead to local houses of worship and groups of believers? Do women have special opportunities and spiritual gifts for bearing witness in an Islamic environment? Is freedom of religious expression the same in a unified religious society as it is in a pluralistic religious society?

What becomes apparent in this accounting is the singularity of bearing witness. Whatever may have been the original intent, circumstances soon made all mission activities subservient to this one purpose. Tensions with local Islamic enthusiasts and opportunistic political leaders came to a climax in the ultimate witness—the martyrdom of Merlin Grove, and the later assassination of several Somalis. Bearing witness for some missionaries included public rebuff, while others were forced to leave the country. Programs were under constant public scrutiny.

While discerning the implications of this situation, while listening carefully to local friends, a daring missiology emerged in the Mennonite work in Somalia. Their task was increasingly defined as "presence." Bearing witness became more and more a return to what one might call traditional Mennonite incarnational servanthood. One believer caught the message: "Jesus became like us Somalis that we might become like him." This peace church struggled to replace any illusory vestiges of the modern notion of "missionary conquest." Deeply committed missionaries and their supporting church decided to permit the teaching of Islam in the Mission schools when the government made this a requirement. One missionary, with the support of colleagues, designed a prayer room on the same school grounds at the suggestion of devout Muslim students. Teachers became public servants when the school property and program were nationalized. When the government ordered the missionaries to leave the country, these church workers wrote a letter to the President of the Republic, thanking him and the Somali people for the privilege of serving there.

Readers will want to reflect on the missiological implications of each vignette in this well-told story. Though no mission situation is ever the same, one can make interesting comparisons between the experiences described here and missions in other times and places. Also, Mennonites were not alone in Somalia. They benefitted and learned from peer groups like the Swedish Lutherans (no longer present), the Sudan Interior Mission, and Roman Catholics who were also learning what it means to be a servant church.

A striking quality of this unpretentious work is the reflection of Somali friends. These reflections demonstrate how respect engenders respect. These friends learned that the Christian gospel deals with all dimensions of life. Incarnational faith has to do with relationships, mutual regard, and a concern for all well-being including education, public health, emergency assistance, and the formation of a peaceful society. One of these friends even quotes the lines of a well-known gospel hymn as "the best definition of Islam there is." While only a few Somalis dared to forsake one faith for another, seeds were planted and have borne fruit not only in Somalia but among Somali people in Kenya, Tanzania, Canada, and the United States.

This graceful book does not pretend to describe or promote a grand scheme for mission. The understated vignettes bear witness to the manner of witness that will increasingly characterize the work of the church in the twenty-first century: long-term commitment rather than short-term expectations; careful listening to local voices; respectful inter-religious relationships; programs and strategies which respond to changing situations; a commitment to peace building amid disorder and hostility; and rediscovering the authenticating character of martyrdom, the last word in "bearing witness."

Readers will surely thank God for those who faithfully, creatively, lovingly, and sacrificially bore witness these fifty years. We also thank God for the many Somali people who befriended these strangers, and provided wise counsel and conspicuous support.

John A. Lapp

Executive Secretary Emeritus of Mennonite Central Committee, and Coordinator of the Global Mennonite History Project for Mennonite World Conference

Preface

Every missionary to Somalia needs a praying and clipping mother like Anna Gehman, Mary Gehman's mother.

These two women clipped from the North American Mennonite press everything published about the Mennonite Mission in Somalia—for 50 years! And mounted the clippings into eight large scrapbooks. Also, they included the onion-skin carbon copies of confidential correspondence between mission administrators at Salunga and their representatives in Mogadishu, when life among the Somalis was more exasperating than delightful, when the mission was thrown into yet one more crisis. And copies of diaries of mission executives and Lancaster bishops on deputation visits to Somalia. Copies, too, of official proclamations handed down by the Somali governments, democratic and revolutionary.

Thus, my work as a researcher for this project was infinitely easier. Most of the documents lay in front of me— thanks to the Gehman women. There were also, of course, the 50 years of administrative files at Salunga to scan.

Often I felt as J. B. Phillips did at work on his paraphrase of the New Testament. In *Ring of Truth*, his testimony of that experience, he writes: "Although I did my utmost to preserve an emotional detachment, I found again and again that the material under my hands was strangely alive." The materials

under my hands were letters, diaries, journals, feature articles, official reports written by missionaries of every profession and psychic disposition, a delightful confluence of characters joined in one mission: to make the way of Jesus the Messiah known among the Somali peoples.

I often felt I was in the presence of something divine as I handled sheets of carbon letters and newspaper clippings. The Somali missionary family underscored that old truth, to quote J. B. Phillips yet again: "It is not usually the atheists and agnostics who are to be found fighting disease, ignorance, and fear in the most dangerous and difficult parts of the world. And this is because the Christian faith, although inevitably rooted in heaven, is incurably earthly. The seeds of this paradoxical attitude are scattered throughout the New Testament."

I am keenly aware that what is written here is chiefly the stories of Mennonites in Somalia, told through Mennonite voices. I do not presume to tell the Somalis' story, how they perceived the presence among them of these Christians called "Mennonites." That story is for Somalis to write, as well as the tragedy of the disintegration of their nation, the suffering of their people—which I have touched on so briefly.

I owe a particular thanks to the book's editorial committee, chaired by Susan Godshall, Representative for Africa, Global Ministries, EMM. Other members included four seasoned Somalia Mennonite missionary alumni: Allen Brubaker, Mary Gehman, Jane Myers Hooley, Harold Reed; and a second generation son of the Mennonite Mission in Somalia, Grant Rissler. While generous with their encouragement, the committee was no rubber stamp. Their suggestions helped refine language appropriate and sensitive for telling this 50-years saga of Mennonites among the Somalis. Also, the counsel of Bertha Beachy and David Shenk was of inestimable value. Stephanie Knudsen of EMM's Communications Department performed the final editing of the manuscript. Thanks to Greg Yoder of that department for the fine graphic design, and Jon Unger Brandt for coordination with the publisher and some editing. Also to be noted with appreciation: the good work of Allen Brubaker and Jane Myers Hooley, with assistance from Dale Gehman (EMM photographer), in culling from hundreds of photographs those published here.

Dear missionary family, once I was one of you, 45 years ago. While the decades have made me a distant relative, still I claim your fine kinship. Reading your lives this past year, I was often deeply touched by your sense of a calling from Christ, your warmth, your unfailing vision in the face of one too many hardships.

I hope I have got down correctly something of your common life together, and with our Somali friends, brothers and sisters. I have been honored by this invitation to put pen to the experiences of your lives.

Omar Eby
Harrisonburg, Virginia
January 2003

Note on this book's spelling of Somali words:

During the Italian presence in Somalia until 1960, Italian spellings are used for places, i.e., Mogadiscio, Chisimaio, and so forth. After independence, the British English spellings are used, i.e., Mogadishu, Kismayu, and so forth. During the literacy campaign of 1972-73, Somali linguists occasionally employed more accurate phonetic spellings. So as not to confuse the reader unnecessarily, these spellings are not used in the text.

Note on the two Mennonite agencies at work in Somalia:

Eastern Mennonite Board of Missions and Charities (EMBMC) serves the Lancaster Conference of Mennonites and other Anabaptist partners. Over 300 long- and short-term missionaries serve in 37 countries. Their offices, west of Lancaster, Pennsylvania, are located in the small town of Salunga. (The popular name, Eastern Mennonite Missions, was adopted in 1993. Throughout the text, references to this agency appear as EMBMC or the Mission Board, and then EMM.)

Mennonite Central Committee (MCC) is the relief, service, community development, and peace organization of the North American Mennonite and Brethren in Christ Churches. Some 1,500 workers serve in 58 countries. Their offices, north of Lancaster, Pennsylvania, are located in the town of Akron.

Note on the names of Somalis:

Due to the sensitive nature of this text, the editorial committee has changed the names of some Somalis mentioned.

Nineteen 50s

Schoolboys Muridi, Shariff, and Ibrahim enjoy reading at Mahaddei, 1950s. *Previous page:* Nur plows with oxen at Torda.

A tree for learning

Carl Wesselhoeft hung up a chalkboard, lined up 20 boys on benches, and called it a school. The chalkboard was a painted piece of masonite; the benches, planks on cement blocks; the school, lacy shade of a thorn tree filled with chittering weaver birds, hanging upside down building nests. Under the tree the boys began to study "the language of birds," as Nur, Carl's early friend and the Mission's night guard, observed: "You people speaking English sound like birds talking!"

"This is a book!" The Somali boys parroted their blond teacher with a long nose. Something new had come to Mahaddei Uen, their village. Mennonites, these kids had never heard of; but Christians, yes. Their Muslim fathers called them *gaal* (infidels). Yet, these same fathers now risked sending their sons to a day school run by Christian missionaries from America.

It was 1956. In March, April, and May, Carl taught in high dry wind. When it rained, the class dashed into the two-room garage apartment behind them. Here Carl lived with Leota and their children: Ruby, Paul, and John. This structure was Leroy Shirk's first; he and his wife Edna lived in a temporary shelter.

Across the next years, Leroy built a three-classroom building, a house for the Wesselhoefts, a house for teacher Mary Gehman and nurse Helen Landis, and a clinic. Later: dormitories for 100 boys ages eight to fifteen, kitchen, dining room, toilets, baths.

Nothing was easy about securing that first outreach, 70 miles north of Mogadiscio. Village elders wanted the school, and they would give land. But politicians said wait until 1960, the date of their national independence from Italy. Egyptian mullahs drove out on Fridays from the capital to oppose these Christians called Mennonites. Yet, 12 acres were granted for 30 years. At the ground-breaking ceremony in December 1955, a clan chief said, "God wills for you to be here!"

Carl Wesselhoeft with first elementary students at Mahaddei, 1956.

A tree for worshiping

Victor and Viola Dorsch sat under a tree with a dozen Somali adults and a dozen children and sang hymns. The hymns were in Swahili, from the songbook *Tenzi za Rohoni*; the seat, a large woven mat of bleached river reeds; the wide tree, a mango, the African peach, its grey-green fruit not yet ripe.

"*Tazama! Tazama! Uishi!*" Tabitha belted out Ira Sankey's "There's Life for a Look at the Crucified One"; others stumbled along, singing lustily, phonetically. The handful of Sunday afternoon worshipers under the mango tree was a tiny remnant of the former Swedish Lutheran Mission endeavors among these riverine peoples, begun in the 1890s. At that time, land southwest of the Juba River belonged to Kenya. But the long finger of European colonialism reached into this remote territory. The Treaty of Versailles reconfigured the border between British Kenya and the Italian Somaliland. In 1935, Mussolini, the Fascist premier in Italy, expelled the Swedish Mission.

Mofi was one of four villages to which the Dorsches made regular visits in 1958. Only a few miles from the Dorsch home at Jamama, Mofi lay across the Juba River. Home to hippos and crocs, the river, wide and chocolately, swelled during the rainy season. To reach Mofi, people floated in a twelve-passenger flat-bottomed boat, navigated by a Somali pulling hand-over-hand on a cable stretched from one river-side to the other. All sat very still and clutched their song and story books about God.

Mofi visits encouraged the Dorsches. In addition to Swahili hymnbooks, they used Swahili phonograph records of simple biblical messages—"interest getters," Victor once described the recordings. Some Sunday afternoons, as many as thirty adults and thirty children strolled into the mango shade to hear stories of Jesus.

Orie O. Miller's vision

But how did Carl Wesselhoeft, a German-born American, and Leota, his Ohio Mennonite wife, come to be teaching under a thorn tree in Somalia? And how did Victor and Viola Dorsch, from Ontario farmland, come to be singing Swahili Sankey by the Juba River in lower Somalia?

Until 1950, Lancaster Mennonites had never heard of Somalia. That January, Orie O. Miller, executive secretary of Eastern Mennonite Board of Missions, returned from a visit to the work in Ethiopia and (then) Tanganyika. He said, "Shouldn't we be interested in Somalia, that country lying in the Horn of Africa?" He said, "Somalis are 99 percent Muslim. In ten years they'll be granted independence."

Eastern Board commissioned two of their veteran Tanganyika missionaries to visit Somalia. In November, Mahlon M. Hess and Dr. Merle Eshleman checked in at an Italian hotel in Mogadiscio. They met salty Indian ocean water on tap for showers, bottled *aqua minerale* and camel roast for dinner, the muggy weather of Mombasa and Dar es Salaam, and the sane institution of siesta. They also met important Italian officials.

Dr. Pier Spinelli, chief of the cabinet and third in the rank of administration, proved most influential. "The Mennonite church must come to Somalia," he said. United Nations officials,

Ivan Yost with Somali friend, 1950s.

too, were helpful, as was an Italian Waldensian Christian in the education department.

Hess and Eshleman wrote, "We recommend: Take immediate steps to establish a mission in the trust territory of Italian Somaliland. . . ." The Eastern Board took that step of faith the next year. Paul N. Kraybill, Orie's right-hand man at Salunga and editor of the *Missionary Messenger*, wrote: "In Somalia we'll face a spiritual battle intensely more difficult than any mission situation in which we've ever found ourselves."

Mahaddei Market, 1950s.

Nomads and camels, politicians and Islam

To travel from crisp Nairobi, the New York of East Africa in the Kenyan highlands, to sweaty Mogadiscio, on the Indian Ocean coastline, is to enter a different world.

To step into the jostle of narrow streets, bazaars heavy with incense and musk, camel caravans, donkey carts, and to hear calls to prayer from minarets, is to enter a Middle Eastern city with all the charm and mystery of the Orient.

Orie O. Miller learned that sandy city lanes ruined the spit-and-polish of his good black shoes. He discovered, too, on his first 265-mile trip from Mogadiscio to Jamama in southern Somalia, how desolate the countryside. "Yesterday was hot, dry, and very dusty," he wrote in his diary. "Indeed, one 99-mile stretch between two villages—all desert with herds of camels feeding on thorn scrub—seemed a long stretch indeed."

Most Somalis live in the arid conditions as Orie and his missionaries saw. "Nomadism is the prevailing economic response," writes I. M. Lewis, a British anthropologist long observant of things Somali. "Their mode of livelihood and social institutions are tightly adjusted to the scant resources of an unenviably harsh environment. . . . The nomadic Somalis are [often] warlike, driven by the poverty of their resources to intense competition for water and grazing."

The phrase "tall, dark, and handsome" might have been invented to distinguish the thin-boned structure of the Somalis. Their near fatalistic trust in the power of Allah and his prophet Muhammad gives some cohesion to a people never united. Their fierce traditional pride shows contempt for their African neighbors. Under the snap of Italy's and the United Nations' flags, Somalis entered yet another phase of alliance and counter-alliance, tilting toward modernity.

Ali feeds a camel near a Torda well, 1950s.

Bert and his Suburban Carryall

Wilbert Lind sat at a sidewalk café in Chisimaio and talked with a Somali man in his early thirties. Bert was on an investigative tour. Somalia's southern port town of white-plastered coral rock had once been home to the Swedish Lutherans. Over spiced *shai* the Somali said, "Yes, I was once a school boy at the Mission. Before they left, nearly twenty years ago." Then, first glancing surreptitiously about, he leaned over their tea and said quietly: "I am still a believer." Again the cautious glance before: "But I have no Bible. Can you help?"

Later, after they parted in the street, Bert turned to look back. He saw the man bowing before a Muslim mullah and kissing the hem of his long cloak.

That afternoon the Italian district commissioner showed Bert the former Swedish Mission compound: an abandoned house, a collapsed schoolroom, a graveyard used as a toilet. But the most heart-wrenching—the four walls of a small church with no roof, its pointed bell-tower raising no cross.

It was late 1953. The Mennonite Mission in Mogadiscio had for six months now settled into its new quarters. Fae Miller and Caroline Plank had joined the Lind family (Rhoda and small son Daniel). Bert was then free to explore Somali towns and villages to find sites for further mission work: medicine, education, and agriculture. He drove the Mission's heavy

Remains of Swedish Lutheran Church building in Chisimaio, abandoned when the Lutheran Mission left Somalia in 1935. The remains as shown were torn down in the 1970s.

tank-like Chevy Suburban Carryall for 2,200 miles over many weeks, looking, talking, praying.

Upriver from Chisimaio, along the Juba, Bert found the remains of Swedish mission stations at other villages: Ionte, Zunguni, Mofi, and Allesandra. He found also a group of brothers and sisters in the faith. He found, too, consolation in Isaiah's divine promise: "He will not break a crushed reed, nor will he snuff out a smoldering wick."

English classes

Fae Miller knew immediately that one of the two women standing at her Mogadiscio apartment door that August afternoon in 1953 was not a Somali. Fae had been in Somalia only six months, but quick-witted and congenial, she accurately read faces and clothing; she heard, too, the woman's tongue stumbling with Somali.

Over tea and biscuits, the middle-aged woman said, "I am a believer from Eritrea. There I knew the Swedish Lutheran missionaries. More than 25 years ago I came to Mogadiscio as a servant of an Italian family."

This Eritrean woman brought other women and children to join the Mennonite missionaries for worship. It was a diverse group by then. Wilbert Lind noted that attendance included: six Protestants, American and Italian; two Greek Orthodox; a Somali Catholic; and eight young Muslim men studying English with him. It would take some months to sort themselves out into several small groups for worship and Bible study.

Needed, too, was Hussen, who had acquired English during the British occupation of World War II. He met his first Mennonites on the occasion of the Hess-Eshleman scout two years previous. Now, he was the Mission's translator. New to him were biblical metaphors. One time translating for Bert, Hussen said, "You can't say 'Lamb of God.' The people will laugh because we don't know what you mean—'Lamb of God'?"

In addition to full schedules teaching English as a second language, Fae and the Linds had many religious classes: Fae with a flannel graph, Rhoda with Mennonite Publishing House Summer Bible school pictures, Bert with Bible stories in simple English.

When Omar Eby arrived mid-1957, he inherited the English classes for men, many students his own age. A young bachelor, he was well-suited for evening and night classes, and for the camaraderie later with students in the city's tea shops.

Fae Miller with women's class in Mogadiscio, 1956.

Mahaddei elementary school students, 1963-64.

Mahaddei Uen: from thorn tree to electric lights

"There's been much opposition to the Mission coming to our village," a Muslim elder, the clan chief for Mahaddei Uen, spoke at the December 1955 ground-breaking ceremony of the Mennonite Mission's elementary school. It was two years to the month since Bert Lind's first visit to this village lying east in a crook of the Shebelli River. "Propaganda was directed against the Mission, asking us not to permit you Christians to come. Other elements tried to persuade you not to come here. But none of those permitted this day from happening. Thus, we believe God wills you to be here."

Three years later, at closing exercises for the school, Mahaddei and Mogadiscio men of influence—the district commissioner, the secretary of the politically powerful Somalia Youth League, the Italian director of schools, clan chiefs, and the village mayor—crammed the program. Everyone wanted a chance publicly to praise the Mennonites. What had happened during the intervening years?

Carl Wesselhoeft, with the assistance of two Somali teachers, one a believer, established the academic quality of their school. Earlier Carl had admitted to impatience toward those to whom he had come to serve. "Now even though they still call us infidels, we love them!" The staff was praised also for its firm yet respectful manner of handling boys—sons of high Mogadiscio government officials, clerks, merchants, and settled peasant farmers. Water on tap and electricity were installed.

Later, Mary Gehman, gentle, indefatigable, joined the team. Nurse Helen Landis (Ali), too, was a teacher. In addition to her four-days-a-week clinic, she taught young men to be medical dressers. Fearless of the African night, she responded at any hour for emergencies; particularly she worried about young wives in their first deliveries. Helen was a Mennonite Nightingale to Mahaddei.

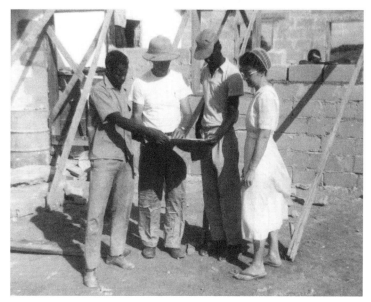
David Miller explains plans for the Mahaddei school building to construction workers and teacher Mary Gehman, 1950s.

Torda: Mennonite Oxboys

Allen Brubaker works with oxen at Torda, 1958.

In a field near Torda, Allen Brubaker strode behind oxen and a steel coulter. It was 1957, and he was far from his dad's Pennsylvania farm with its Holstein cows, silos, and draft horses. Allen applied his horse sense to train oxen to plow, a rarity in Somalia, whose agricultural economy was either the hand hoe of Somali peasantry or the diesel tractor of Italian irrigated banana plantations. He also trained the Somali chief's son to plow with Samson and Bozo, the Mennonite oxen. Chester Kurtz and Marvin Musser rounded out the team of farm boys at Torda.

Torda, twelve miles below the Equator, a rural village of 300 people, swelled to 800 during the wet season, the months for cultivation. The agricultural scheme had the blessing of the Somali government, which tried constantly to woo the nomads of the interior to settle by the river basins, pick up a hoe, and learn farming. But centuries of moving camel herds to follow the rains bred in the herdsmen a disdain for manual labor. It was something for their riverine neighbors.

So, Samson and Bozo were "appropriate technology" of late 1950s vintage, introduced by Mennonite farmboys long before the concept became the rallying mantra of the second wave of United States development officers. Oxen economy fit appropriately between the hoe and the tractor. Still, the Mennonite boys were modest: "So far, we're the ones who're learning the most." These PAX boys—as commonly referred to—were conscientious objectors to war who sought alternative service, first in reconstruction in Europe after WWII, later in agriculture and rural development on other continents, including Africa.

Not only oxen were introduced. The PAX boys established two two-acre plots. One worked at dry farming, relying on the rainy season; the other used irrigation to water vegetable and papaya gardens. They dug a pit silo to demonstrate the storage green maize. The boys taught English and gave teas in their mud-and-wattle cottage.

From Margherita to Jamama

Not only was old Margherita getting a new name, Jamama was getting new residents—North American Christians called Mennonites.

In July 1957, a three-vehicle convoy moved the Shirks and the Dorsches to rented quarters in Jamama, 265 miles south of Mogadiscio. The chief of police and the district commissioner dropped in on the missionaries as they unloaded their trucks. "We welcome you," they said, and immediately added, "When are you going to open an English school?"

Yet, three weeks later, a Muslim priest at Friday prayers organized a large group of people to protest the coming. Their approach to the Mennonite house was intercepted by the police. He turned them to the district commissioner's office. "We protest the coming of Christian missionaries!" they cried. The next morning the commissioner came to assure Victor Dorsch with a warm handshake and best wishes, "The national constitution calls for religious freedom. I am here to establish that law with order." Thanking God again for that reassurance, the missionaries fell to work.

Roy Shirk built a garage-apartment-workshop, two houses, a clinic, and a three-room school. The Dorsches began English classes for adults and hosted a deputation of Tanganyika Mennonite pastors and missionaries to explore teaching in Swahili-speaking villages. Fae Miller, the teacher of English and Somali, now could practice her training as a nurse. Newly arrived Bertha Beachy, ebullient and confident, unpacked elementary school aids in classrooms still smelling of fresh cement. David Miller, an Iowa widower and builder, apprenticed with Roy Shirk; building a clinic on Somalia's spongy black cotton soil was nothing like erecting a hog barn on Midwestern loam.

Easter, a year later: a group of Somalis sat in the new Dorsch house. Many for the first time heard stories about Jesus' suffering, death, and resurrection.

Group of friends, Jamama, 1959.

Weeping and rejoicing

It was the darkest hour of an African night, October 1959. Rhoda Lind lay alone in her Mogadiscio bed; her husband Wilbert lay sick with hepatitis in a Nairobi hospital. Rhoda startled awake. She barely made out the form of a man above her. Disguised in aprons and housecoats, the assailant waved a weapon threateningly above her face. Rhoda struck out to defend herself and sliced her thumb on a butcher knife. With uncommon strength she thrust off the intruder and staggered to her feet. "Wait," she said, "I'll get money." Only then did she realize that she was bleeding profusely about the face where she had been sliced in her sleep. Still she did not scream, even when he tapped on her side with the point of his knife.

When she turned around, the man was gone. In the kitchen, Rhoda found the door open, a glass pane at the lock broken, the butcher knife missing. The kitchen clock said 2:15 a.m. Finding the telephone wires cut, she rang her brass table bell and called loudly into the dead night. American neighbors arrived to give her care. The next day, Somali students hearing of the attack came by to give apologies and condolences; some wept, grieved that anyone should attack the Mennonites. "The Lord is my shield. My heart trusted him, and I am helped," Rhoda said, quoting the psalmist. The American community pooled money to fly Rhoda to Nairobi for surgery and rest.

Wilbert and Rhoda Lind in Somalia Mennonite office, Mogadiscio, 1950s.

Yet, two months earlier the Mennonite family had gathered in joy. At a special service in Jamama, former believers were again united in fellowship. Nationals and missionaries confessed sin, wept, and dedicated themselves afresh. All then gathered at the Lord's table and washed each other's feet. With that, the fellowship of Somali believers was reborn.

At the end of this decade the nation, too, awaited its birth as the Republic of Somalia—July 1, 1960—another occasion for joy.

I remember...

Billie Musse Shemal
Former District Commissioner
Margherita/Jamama

I remember... when Wilbert Lind in late 1953 first came to southern Somalia. We happened to meet at a hotel restaurant in Chisimaio. We talked together for a length of time. I knew about Protestant missions from my earlier contact with the Swedish Lutheran Mission when I was a boy. I knew that Christian missionaries would help my people. So, I invited the Mennonite Mission to come settle in Chisimaio. But I heard nothing from Mr. Lind for a few years.

I remember... when Chester Kurtz and Marvin Musser—PAX boys, they were called—Mennonite farmboys, came to the Juba Valley in 1956. They went to the village of Torda, a dozen miles below the Equator, where they helped in agriculture. I saw that the purpose of their mission was clear—to help my people. Then I again met Mr. Lind.

I remember... when I was district commissioner in Margherita in 1957, I first met Victor and Viola Dorsch who moved into a rented house in the town—now called Jamama. They helped in education; later medical assistance followed. These people, too, were good: they were interested in my people; they helped my people.

I remember... shortly after the Mennonites moved to Jamama, renting Nur Costelli's house, a group of townspeople came to my office to protest. The instigators of the demonstration didn't want the Christian Mission in their town. As their district commissioner, I told them it was illegal to march in a protest. I threatened to report them to Mogadiscio authorities. I told them that these Mennonites were no different than the earlier Swedish missionaries who had once worked in Ngambo and Mofi villages across the river. With that the protest was peacefully settled. I assured the people the Mennonite schools would have good teachers.

I remember... when my Somali people learned to trust the Mennonite missionaries. These people learned our Somali language and related well with the village people. They often talked with them and visited us in our homes. We saw that they came to help us. This was proven by the many times the Mennonites transported sick people from Jamama to a hospital in Chisimaio with the Mission's Land Rover. This was before the Jamama Hospital was built.

I remember... when a man I knew in town wanted the safest place to protect his money. He took it to the Mennonites to be kept in the Mission safe. Other people did the same, trusting the Mennonite safe deposit, and its keeper, Victor Dorsch.

I remember. . . when I was once helpful to the PAX boys. They rode from Torda to Jamama on their bicycles late one afternoon. From my commissioner's office I saw them peddle by. I told one of the police officers to go and ask the American boys what they were doing. Chester and Marvin reported that they had come to town to get their mail and have supper with the Dorsches. Then they'd bicycle back to Torda. The policeman told them that the district commissioner wanted to see them at his office before they returned. Later, when the PAX boys came by my office, I told them it wasn't safe for them to ride to Torda at that late hour. I feared for their safety, so I sent for my driver and vehicle to take them home. I told them never to do that again!

I remember. . . years later, possibly 1971, I came from Chisimaio to see the mission doctor at Jamama Hospital. This was my first visit; I had never met the doctor. An Arab, waiting in the line, introduced me to the mission doctor—he treated me immediately.

I remember. . . all those good people at the Mennonite Mission in Jamama.

Toronto, Canada
October 2002

Nineteen 60s

The Arba Rucun Mosque in Mogadiscio, with cathedral in background, 1967.

Long live Somalia!

"*Somalia ha nolato!*" three million Somalis cried. "Long live Somalia!" Villages and cities pulsed with amplified music and giddy visions. "We'll govern ourselves! We'll have our own alphabet! We'll have an air force! We'll all drive cars! Sinclair will find oil! Allah will bless us!" Mennonites joined the celebrations.

July 1, 1960, the Somali Republic was born. The former Italian Somaliland and the former British Somaliland merged their separate legislatures to make the latest republic on the African continent. Several presidential candidates emerged in the South, the North, and the joint body: Abdullahi Issa, Mohammed Ibrahim Egal, Aden Abdullah Osman, and Abd ar-Rashid Ali Shermarke. Spotlights blazed on the new flag, a pale blue field with a large lone white star.

The five points of that star became an image for political rally. Like nationals all over Africa, Somalis talked ambitiously of redrawing the borders imposed by white men a hundred years ago. Haji Mohammed Hussein, whom *Time* magazine branded "an oldtime nationalist rabble-rouser," first cried for a union of all Somalis. Although jailed for a bloody disturbance, his oratory was infectious. Now all politicians clamored for a united Somalia. So far only two points of their star—former Italian Somaliland and former British Somaliland—were joined. Somali nomads also roamed the fertile regions of northern Kenya, and the Ogaden of eastern Ethiopia. Greater Somalia's fifth star point included French Somaliland and its deep-water port. But they had only recently opted to remain with old DeGaulle. "France is here and intends to stay," he said.

Did any new nation face bleaker prospects than the Somali Republic? The world's news magazines wondered. Dry, sun-blasted, largely a scrub desert. Her assets—1.3 million camels and goats and a cadre of capable, moderate leaders who bore no grudge against the West. The World Bank gave six million dollars a year to help keep the new republic afloat. Others saw great hope for a people united by language, religion, and history.

Students of the Islamic Cultural Center parade on Independence Day, Mogadiscio, 1960.

Suspicion, opposition, and grace

"Cease all activities." The command was blunt, the speakers congenial. Policemen summoned Wilbert Lind to appear before Mogadishu officials. The ban—March 24, 1962—came down from the Council of Ministers. Policemen delivered the message orally at Mahaddei; at Jamama, a written notice. Rumors swept the towns: Wesselhoeft had baptized 21 Somali school boys in the Shebelli River. The Mission had ordained Somali priests in Jamama. New Somali believers distributed Arabic Gospel tracts in Mogadishu.

Conservative Muslim mullahs, influenced by Egyptian missionaries, had agitated against the Mennonites. Eventually Lind and Harold Stauffer met with the minister of foreign affairs to affirm their cooperation. Later they learned that only the last charge was true; zealous new believers gave out Christian literature in Mogadishu markets. Three days later the Linds left for a furlough in the United States. Merlin Grove, fearful yet capable, was appointed director.

"We appreciate your Mission's social services," the minister of education said to Grove and Wesselhoeft a month later. "But we are against the basic things for which you stand. You use intellectual subtlety to undermine the simple faith of the masses, to win converts to your faith. Unless you stay clear of all ecclesiastical activities, we'll not let you reopen your schools."

David Miller, builder, with his motorcycle, 1950s.

About the same time, Victor Dorsch in Jamama had a chance meeting in a restaurant with the district commissioner and the governor. Pressed, the two said, "Go ahead, open the hospital." Two weeks later Mahaddei officials lifted restrictions against the clinic. But another month passed before the government addressed the matter of the closed Mennonite Mission schools. Finally, July 5, three days after a private meeting with the prime minister, Grove received verbal permission to open all schools. "These days we've been thrown fully into God's hands," Merlin wrote.

Murder and forgiveness

He sat quietly among parents waiting to register students for the Mahaddei Primary School, July 1962. Fondling a dagger under the folds of his clerical robe, the Somali mullah sought this opportune moment to rid his country of the *gaal* (infidels), the Mennonite Mission.

The Somali Government had just given permission for the Mission schools to reopen after several months' closure. But extreme agitation began when a declared believer distributed Arabic copies of Mark's Gospel on the streets of Mogadishu. Several clerics in the mosques then preached violence against the Mission.

Merlin Grove sat at a table registering students while Harold Stauffer, his back turned, prepared textbooks for sale. Suddenly, dagger drawn, the mullah sprang upon Merlin, fatally stabbing him in the chest. He then turned toward Harold, who fled for the nearly blocked exit.

Pursuing Harold and shouting words of praise to Allah, the assassin spotted Dorothy, Merlin's wife, rushing toward the office, drawn there by the commotion. He turned upon her—stabbing her three times in the abdomen before students could pull him away.

Dorothy lived, and from her hospital bed, expressed love and forgiveness for the Somali people. Later, at the assassin's trial, Harold Stauffer spoke for the Mission the official words of forgiveness. The government and people of Somalia denounced the act of violence and declared appreciation for the work of the Mennonite Mission.

Two infants in the Mission family preceded Merlin in death, both by illness: Evelyn Wesselhoeft, January 1958, and Peter John Leaman, 1960. David Miller, a builder, died two years later in a road accident.

Merlin and Dorothy Grove with children, Bruce, Pauline, and David, 1960.

Christmas: whispered joy

"No, sir," the man in Johar said to David Shenk, "No one here celebrates Christmas!" With steel in his eyes and pride in his voice, he nearly spat a curse. "*Festo o gaal*—the festival of God-blasphemers! The holiday for European drunkards!" The villager did not know that a small group of believers gathered quietly on the edge of his town to celebrate the Incarnate God.

Nor would he know that on Christmas Eve, Elsie VanPelt, Fae Miller, and the Wesselhoeft family drove 40 miles into the bush beyond Mahaddei to have a Christmas picnic and worship. A Somali friend, with his wife and children, went along. Roasted goat meat, bread, and tea were heated over the camp fire. Then, with Christmas card pictures, the Somali told the Christmas story to his wife and children. He prayed: "O God, here we are in the bush. We have no stick, no gun, no dagger. We have only you to protect us. We trust in you."

At a Christmas gathering in Mogadishu, they sang a new hymn composed by one of them: "Although snow and hyenas assault me, I will not deny my Saviour." One person said, "Jesus became like us Somalis that we might become like him." At Jamama, Viola Dorsch and Mary Ellen Leaman sewed weekly with village women—the Kadijas and Mariams and Fatimas. These women knew about Jesus born of Mary, a story in the Qur'an. The prayer for them was to find their peace in him.

By Christmas, six months after the death of Merlin Grove and copious condolences from the prime minister and students, missionary life settled into normal routines, pleasant and busy. School boys and girls again hunched over math books; adults in the night school learned to spell the nonphonetic English; hundreds of sick villagers visited the clinics; the Somali Nicodemuses quietly resumed their studies. Some celebrated their first Christmas in 1962.

Market scene, 1960s.

From Torda to Noleye

Somalis with *aqals* (nomadic houses) loaded on camels, 1960s.

"Smile at the thorns scratching the jeep, laugh at the sun burning down, love the elephants that tramped up and down the muddy roads. Then, wind on a foot-path between scrub bush. Three flat tires. Stuck in a mud hole at night. Three days later, the tiny Noleye village settlement of Bartire nomads. [Yusuf] had returned with a Land Rover and two white boys. People gathered quickly. The sheik offered tea and roasted corn.

Young boys danced our welcome." So wrote Raymond Martin in 1962. The other white boy was Daniel Stoltzfus, the last PAX boy, who along with Ivan Yost phased out the agriculture demonstration efforts at Torda.

Two years earlier, Yusuf, a believer, came to the Mennonites with a vision—help settle his 30,000 nomadic people. Start with a village of 30 huts and oxen plows on his clan's land west of the Juba River. Thus began the Mission's second venture in agriculture. But again, not in ignorance. Paul Kraybill wrote, "Care will be needed to avoid the temptation to transplant American equipment and civilization." Newly minted anthropologist Don Jacobs arrived from Tanganyika to survey the people and their land, and he drew up a modest proposal.

But later, the Noleye leader brought such harsh accusations against Raymond, he had to leave. Fortunately, Chester and Catherine Kurtz were also in Noleye. They joined a few of Yusuf's clansmen to continue work at the settlement, work first begun by Raymond: build a house, a village store, and a small ferry boat; clear an air strip; plant corn fields and vegetable gardens. Yusuf erected a small chapel under heavy trees by the river. But the nomads did not forsake their camel herds. Not even 30 families participated.

The next year, 1964, found Chester teaching math, science, and music at the Johar middle school; Catherine as a nurse aide cared for sick school boys.

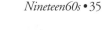

Books and bedpans boom

"Yes, it's unusual to see a female shopkeeper. But I want experience. I like people. I like books. I want to go abroad and study journalism." The clerk behind the counter of New Africa Booksellers split her time between selling Oxford English Readers for Africa and chatting with a reporter from the weekly English Somali News. The woman speaking could have been Bertha Beachy, manager of the Mission's bookshop on Parliament Square—but it was her Somali assistant.

Headmaster David Shenk stood by the flagpole at Shebelli Intermediate School, Johar, before 160 boys and their teachers, Chester and Catherine Kurtz and Mary Gehman. He reminisced, "Four years earlier, 1963, forty-five boys were crammed into one dorm with salty water. Things are much better now. More dorms, more classrooms, clean water, good Somali teachers. We haven't had a student riot in five months!" And the believer group increased.

In Jamama, the Mennonite Mission hospital provided much-needed medical care for people from Chisimaio to Gelib. An audience of 300 gathered for the dedication of the new 25-bed hospital. Townspeople and dignitaries milled with the staff: Hershey Leaman, hospital administrator; Dr. Ivan Leaman; Fae Miller, R.N.; Ali Osman, a Somali nurse. Later, Dr. Harold Housman, "the miracle doctor" from Tanzania, used his scalpel to restore sight to 21 folks with cataracts.

The cable read: "Two Million Shillings Donated to Build Secondary School at Johar"—a gift from West German church organizations. The Dorsches moved to Kismayu, ten years after the Mission had first been rejected. The English night school with nearly 500 students kept Victor and Viola busy from 3:00 p.m. to 9:00 p.m. The 1960s boomed for the Mennonites. Yet these "Golden Years," as the Somalis call this decade, ended with a political assassination and a military coup.

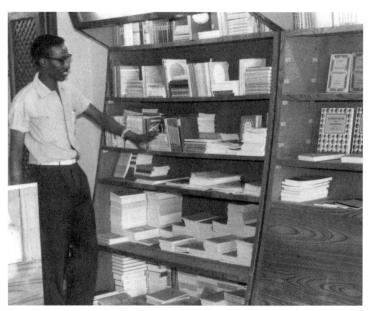

Hussein at New Africa Booksellers, 1967.

Constitutional changes challenge Christians

"It shall not be permissible to spread or propagandize any religions other than the True Religion of Islam." With that one-sentence amendment to Article 29 (Freedom of Religion), the National Assembly of the Somali Republic, three years after independence, unanimously ratified their national constitution on June 1963. Article 29 had read: "Every person shall have the right to freedom of conscience and freely to profess his own religion and to practice its rites." Dr. Ahmed Darman, Somali representative to the United Nations, declared, "The amendment underscores Islam as the state religion but does not impinge on the internal activities of other religions."

"If I want to study the Bible, how can my government keep me from that?" Twenty-two bright Somali chaps in Mogadishu spoke aloud their disbelief before each other assembled for weekly worship. With risk, and emboldened by the Holy Spirit, believers still met.

Three months later, yet another challenge. The government required the "teaching of Islam in private schools as well as public." Not only were the Mennonites not allowed to teach their Christian faith in their own private schools, now they must provide Islam in their curriculum, taught by Somalis. What should they do? The Sudan Interior Mission closed its schools rather than cooperate.

Lena Horning (Brown) teaches at Jamama, 1967.

With discussion, correspondence, prayer; with Orie Miller's and Paul Kraybill's leadership; with the unanimous agreement of the believers and missionaries; the Lancaster Conference bishops, with fasting and prayers, and the Mission Board stamped their approval: "To permit religious instruction in Islam in our schools in Somalia." Mission schools would thereby become model schools implementing the Somali government curriculum.

A year later (1964) Paul Kraybill noted, "This action has not compromised our witness. In fact, it has helped to break down negative attitudes that hindered."

Somali woman in Mogadishu, 1969.

Famine relief and nursing education

"The camp of 10,000 victims of poverty, drought, and starvation chokes one with tears." Dr. Ivan Leaman, fresh back (in May 1965) from the United States for a second term, was immediately assigned to Galcaio. The town of 10,000 lay 500 road miles north of Mogadishu. The year-long drought with subsequent malnutrition and related diseases seemed unabated as it doubled the population. Various nations responded with food and medicines. Only after the departure of three U.S. Army medical units did the Somali government invite the Mennonite Mission to help.

"The hospital was crowded with pneumonia and dysentery patients," Dr. Ivan wrote. Among those one morning he met a father and mother who had walked 40 miles, carrying three children too ill to walk. "They had nine children, but six had already died." Dan Wert, Jr., a registered nurse fresh from an assignment in Honduras, joined Dr. Leaman for six weeks. "I ate meals from cans bearing labels from Kenya, Italy, Britain, the U.S., Paraguay, Australia, China—part of the relief aid."

At the other end of Somalia, an official from the Ministry of Health addressed guests at the May 1968 opening ceremony of the Jamama Hospital Nurse-Dresser School. "Man is not just a piece of paper that can be thrown away," he said. Six Somali men and two women comprised the first class for the two-year course. Esther Mack (King), the director, taught pharma-cology, nutrition, and public health; Miriam Leaman (Segerstrom), surgical nursing and first aid; Anna Lutz (Lehman), maternal child care; Dr. Leaman, medicine. UNICEF gave student stipends, equipment, and teaching aids. After classes the students scattered to various posts throughout the hospital to gain practical experience. Saida: "I helped in my first delivery!" Abdullahi: "I dressed the leg of a small boy suffering extreme pain from a poisonous snake bite." Salah: "I screened patients' symptoms; should they see the doctor or a nurse?"

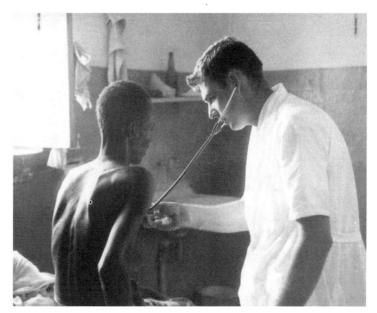

Dr. Ivan Leaman with patient, when he assisted in famine relief at Galcaio, 1965.

Religious conversation

Leon Good studies with Hussein, 1970.

"I have been informed that religious functions are taking place at Mennonite missions at which Somali citizens are receiving teaching in the Christian religion. I cannot permit Somali persons to attend non-Muslim rites."
The Somali Minister of State's October 1964 letter to Bert Lind was blunt. What indeed was going on?

Since the early 1950s, young Mogadiscio men had come to inquire about religion and occasionally join in worship. Some asked missionaries to help them study the Bible. The workers honored requests only if they were put into writing. Lydia Glick (Samatar) told of many religious discussions, particularly with a student who was a missionary for Islam.

In the 1960s, it seemed that every Mennonite missionary had been asked by Somalis for help studying the Bible. At Mahaddei, a 104-year-old remnant of Africa's slave-raiding days, an aging few, came to the Wesselhoeft house for worship. Students, teachers, and workmen attended various Bible studies. Seven men begged Merlin Grove for instruction in the Scriptures. Mary Gehman received a plaintive note from a student: "I'd like to learn the Bible stories, but classmates said they'd tell my father. If he hears he'll take me out of school."

At Jamama, a friend told Fae Miller, "I've watched you missionaries for three years. Now I want to show the Light of Jesus to my own people. Victor Dorsch reported, "The believers here have elected three mature elders." And at Kismayu, Somalis expressed their interest in Bible study and worship as soon as the Dorsches moved to that southern town.

By the end of the 1960s, many Mennonite missionaries studied the Bible with Somalis, individually or in small groups. Whispers of new wind were beginning to blow in this dry land.

Assassination, military coup, and a Revolutionary Council

John Zook, builder of the secondary school at Johar, with his family and Mary Gehman, jolted along the road south to Mogadishu. He needed another load of supplies. But, at the sand dunes just outside the capital, armed soldiers blocked access to the city. With the slam of their car door, the Zook passengers heard the grinding of metal gears. The tanks' turrets leveled their long guns at their car. "Turn back!" the soldiers said. "Don't ask questions!"

Back at Johar the missionaries already had answers, news received from town—a military coup occurred in Mogadishu. Tanks rolled in the streets. Two days previous, a gunman assassinated President Shermarke as he toured the drought-stricken regions of northern Somalia. Fewer than 24 hours after the state burial of the president, a self-styled revolutionary council seized power without bloodshed. They disbanded the democratically elected parliament; they placed the president's cabinet under house arrest; they slapped a curfew on the capital. Somalia was having its own October Revolution, but in 1969. The young officers of the coup triggered events which led to the rise of Somalia's own brand of Bolshevism.

"October 21, 1969, shall be held as a sacred day," the *Mogadishu Somali News* crowed. "The National Army accomplished a holy service to the nation. You saved our sacred land from the vicious hands of money grabbers and oppressors. We enter a new era with hearts throbbing with joy. Political bribery, tribalism, nepotism, and misappropriation of public money are over once and forever."

More detached observers attributed the coup to popular frustration with the parliamentary system bogged down in ancient clan rivalries, with high unemployment, and a worsening drought. Major-General Mohamed Siad Barre emerged as the revolutionary leader. He reigned for twenty-two years as a dictator.

A camel caravan, 1950s.

Outdoor market at Brava, a coastal town in Somalia, 1960.

The Gullet

Mohamud S. Togane

    We Somalis have failed
to listen,
to learn
the lesson the Mennonites have been trying to teach us
for the last fifty years:
to love God and to love each other.
That is why today the Somali nation is homeless;
that is why we Somalis have made our home
Somalia
into a hell to flee from.
Not only have we Somalis failed
to listen,
to learn that lesson,
we Somalis have also killed
on July 16, 1962
one of the Mennonite teachers
who came to teach us Somalis that lesson:
Merlin Russell Grove.
Right now,
in my mind's eye,
in the village of Mahaddei Uen
I can see Merlin
I can even hear Merlin

singing
as it was his wont
the best definition of Islam there is:
Perfect submission, perfect delight,
Visions of rapture now burst on my sight;
Angels descending bring from above
Echoes of mercy, whispers of love.
Perfect submission, all is at rest,
I in my Saviour am happy and blest;
Watching and waiting, looking above,
    Filled with His goodness, lost in His love.
This is my story.
This is my song,
Praising my Saviour all the day long.
    This message of the Word of Love
    This message of the Prince of Peace
    This message of Jesus
    that
    Merlin and his fellow Mennonites have been trying to teach
us Somalis
    for the last fifty years
    is no different
    from the message
    Weel-waal too tried to teach us Somalis
    ages ago.

Will we Somalis ever listen
Will we Somalis ever learn

their message of
"What Makes Men Dwell Together in Peace."

Weel-waal,
   King of the Darod Bartire clan,
   one of the rarest ornaments of the Somali race,
   called for a powwow with his braves
   and
   addressed them thus:
   "I want you to return to your homes;
   I want each one of you to kill the best lamb of his flock
   and
   come back on the morrow with the part of the animal
   that makes men either brothers or enemies."
   When the morrow dawned,
   one brave brought the royal shoulder
   so-called because it is served
   to royalty,
   to heroes,
   to honored guests.
   Another brave brought a good saddle of mutton;

another brought a leg;
another brought the ribs;
another brought liver;
but when Omar brought out the gullet,
they blurted out
in dismay
in disgust
in chorus:
"What an egregious insult!
What a heel!
What a heller!
What a hellion!
What an awful hellhound
to offer an offal
to the father of us all
to the king of us all!"

But Weel-waal smiled,
   saluting Omar
   as the wisest sage
   as the savviest son of a gun of the Somalis
   saying,
   "Omar is right-on:
   The gullet is the symbol of selflessness:

The gullet is that part of the animal
that makes men either brothers or enemies.
The gullet receives the food first;
but the gullet is most selfless;
like my mother who always ate our leftovers;
the gullet chooses to eat last;
the gullet does not hoard the food;
the gullet does not hog the food;
the gullet is guileless;
the gullet is guiltless;
the gullet is no greedy gut at all!
The gullet passes the food down;
the gullet downs the food
sending it down
down to each and every part of the body
awaiting
all the while
Patiently
for her fair share.

O man of greed and graft,
   go for it;
   go the distance;
   go to the mat;

go for broke;
go to the gullet;
consider her ways and be wise.
So long as men share
fair and square
as the gullet
they dwell together
like us
in peace:
and
behold
how good
how pleasant
it is
when brothers
like us
dwell together
in unity;
but how can there be peace
when one SOB seizes power and pelf
eating alone
gloating
slobbering silly and sick
bloating with pride

playing with his seven insatiable bellies of unbelief
in the Grace of God
growing fat
growing forgetful
growing slick
growing sleek as a seal
hoarding
hogging
living
high on the hog
looking like the pig he is
oinking like the pig he is
rooting up his own grave with his own snout
like the pig he is
while the awful long sharp nagging needles of hunger
are leaching life out of his neighbor?
Omar!
The more words I weave,
the more miserable you make your mien, why?"

    "Alas, My King!
    The praise you have just heaped upon me
    belongs to my fifteen-year-old lass,
    Sophia,
    who prevailed upon me to bring you the gullet!"

"Glory be to God!
    There is no power nor strength nor wisdom save in God!
then Sophia is the wisest Somali sage!"

Toronto, Canada
September 2002

I dedicate this poem to my beloved English teacher, Mary Gehman, who taught this Caliban* in the benighted bush of Mahaddei more than her language: who taught me how to mine the meaning and the marrow of poetry. —M.S.T.

*Caliban, "a savage and deformed" subhuman character, appears in Shakespeare's *The Tempest*. A representative manifestation of wild untamed nature, Caliban is "a natural man." He learns to speak—not only to curse—but to rise to lyrical poetry. Shakespeare accords him some of the loveliest lines of the play. In the end he recognizes his folly and expresses his intention to improve himself in a religious metaphor: he will "seek for Grace."

Nineteen 70s

John Zook explains Shebelli Secondary School plan to students, 1971. *Previous page:* Sowing field for corn, Shebelli Secondary School, Johar, 1973.

An Eternal Memorial

Only months after the military coup, a Mennonite missionary stood with a general of the Revolutionary Council before a 30-foot slender obelisk in a grove of trees in downtown Johar. The Chinese smiled, the Russians smiled, the Mennonites smiled. Somali men clapped, Somali women yodeled, Somali children danced. The monument's inscription read: ETERNAL MEMORIAL, OCTOBER 21, 1969. A salute to Somalia's first step toward progressive socialism. The builder: Mennonite missionary John Zook. His reward: a commission to erect fifteen office buildings, five meat and vegetable markets, a slaughterhouse, a public bath, and a fresh water well. The Johar mayor said, "We've learned to trust Zook."

Zook's steady nerve was amply demonstrated on the edge of Johar. There with a $300,000 budget—a gift from German churches—and a crew of 90 Somali men, he supervised the construction of 21 buildings, the Mennonite Mission's Shebelli Secondary School. "It's the quietest construction project I've ever been on," Zook said. "Few power tools or motorized equipment. Above the splat of wet mortar and the plop of fresh cement, I heard Somalis singing rhythmic work songs."

As Zook neared completion of the new campus, a delegation of Muslim secondary school boys came to him with a request: "Build us a place of prayer." After deliberation and prayer, the Mission Council gave permission. The Nairobi-based architect designed a small mosque, positioned to face Mecca, which fit the architectural landscape. Now Muslim students also had a place of worship. A few years earlier, believing students at Shebelli School had remained on campus during a school break to participate in a discipleship training institute. Afternoons they worked together to fix up a garage between two staff apartments for a place of worship. "This spirit of respect for one another, which EMBMC nurtured, helped to build trust, and was greatly appreciated by the Somali people," noted David Shenk, the Shebelli headmaster.

Painting of memorial in Johar built by John Zook.

A highway for Christmas

Midnight and Christmas Eve, 1971. The Southern Cross hung low out of the black sky. A thick silence lay over the vast interior scrubland. The immense space swallowed the thonk of camel bell and the distant throb of the camp generator. Two men sat sipping coffee. Blanketed by the silent night they seemed to whisper as they talked. One was a German engineer; the other, a Mennonite missionary.

David Shenk drove on a fresh scar through the bush to a German road-building camp 100 kilometers from any Somali village. David was to conduct a midnight service. "Why did you invite me?" he asked his tall German host.

The engineer studied his own thoughts for several minutes. Then: "My work is development. The highway you traveled to get here is the best in the Horn of Africa. We're blazing this extension of technology into the hinterland, hoping it will stimulate agricultural settlements. I've worked at this sort of thing for 20 years. I believe Christmas has a lot to do with this type of human development."

"Yes!" David said. "Christmas has something to do with turning a track into a highway, and bushland into farmland!" This was no longer coffee cup chitchat.

Returning the next morning to his school at Johar, David, always a preacher, felt a sermon shaping in his mind—Develop-ment in light of the Christmas event: "Christian conscience tempers the uses man puts to technology; indeed it must be so, for technology without conscience is demonic. If development is community, as anthropologists say, then the missionary has a calling to help people in community. Without the tempering effect of a commonwealth, economic progress can dissipate into the selfishness of the privileged few." The Incarnate God introduced love into human relationships, and thus, exploitive capitalism can be restrained. As Isaiah wrote, "Clear a highway across the desert for our God!"

David Shenk (right), interim director of Somalia Mennonite Mission, hands over responsibilities to Harold Reed, 1970.

Ag missions: Act III, Mahaddei

Maize, peanuts, sesame, sorghum, cotton, and a German experimental wheat lay green over the small fields. Tomatoes, peppers, eggplant, lettuce, cabbage, cauliflower, melons, cucumbers, radishes, turnips, kohlrabi, and red beets studded the gardens. All were irrigated from the nearby Shebelli River. Ginger, a part-German shepherd dog, assigned to frighten away the herbivorous, nocturnal hippopotami, patrolled the banks. Leon and Elaine Good, Lancaster Mennonite agricultural missionaries, stood with Somali peasant farmers and looked on all that their hands had wrought. This first full-time community development couple for Mahaddei lay a solid foundation. By 1972 the elementary school boys were gone. Their old classrooms now stored farm and garden tools, seeds and a pump.

"The Mahaddei region situated along the Shebelli has rich agricultural land," Leon observed. "My first efforts were to train oxen to till the soil. All went well, but they succumbed easily to the disease carried by the tsetse fly which infests this area."

This third attempt by the Mennonites at agricultural development also had the government's blessings. Brigadier General Hussen Kulmie, vice president of the Somali Revolutionary Council, the year previous had met with Harold Reed. "We welcome the Mennonite Mission's cooperation with the government's efforts at Mahaddei." As with John Zook at

Leon Good and Yusuf inspect vegetable seed packets at Mahaddei, 1973.

Johar, the government here, too, had a grand scheme for the Mennonite Mission: dig a huge canal off the Shebelli River to the interior for transportation and irrigation. Kulmie went on to say, "Our Council's endorsement is crucial when traditional village leaders resist change."

After six locations in three East African countries, the Bob and Betty Buckwalter family welcomed Mahaddei as home. Replacing Good as director of the farming demonstrations, Bob added extension work, covering a 30-mile radius.

Shots in the night

The insistent knocks were loud on the headmaster's door at Johar that night in 1971. Grace Shenk wondered aloud, "Who at this late hour?" Excited school boys talked at once. "Someone died of cholera in Johar! We must all get shots tonight!" David Shenk motorscootered into town for a calmer report. He discovered medical personnel vaccinating against cholera. The school boys were right.

On return to the mission house, he handed Leona Myer two vials of cholera vaccine. "Well, it looks like your work is cut out for tonight!" But Leona was aghast. The tiny school clinic was for emergency first aid. She had only several needles and syringes. How could she violate her knowledge of medical asepsis and give unsterile injections? Quickly they threw together an assembly line clinic for the seventy-five boys. Teachers became medics: David typed up names and ages; Mary Gehman cleaned arms with alcohol; Everett, Leona's husband, sterilized needles. Leona, the left-handed nurse, gave the shots. They finished by midnight.

This was not the only mass vaccination against death-threatening cholera the Mission joined. The medical team at Jamama Hospital gave 10,257 shots over a two-month period. At Mahaddei, Fae Miller gave over 600 to villagers and people in the outlying bush. She also aided Musa, a recent graduate of the nurse-dresser program of the Jamama Hospital. He was in

Miriam Leaman (Segerstrom) and Kadija, nurses at nurses' station, Jamama Hospital, 1964.

charge of the isolation tents for cholera patients set up outside the village.

With the arrival of Velma Eshleman (Nzesi), R.N., public health at Mahaddei got an additional boost. With her certified nurse's assistant, Ali, they spent four days a week on dusty paths. In a radius of 60 miles, they visited three villages to the east of Mahaddei, six to the south, three to the west, seven to the north. At some stops they contacted nomads from the interior who came for water and supplies.

Esther Mack (King) teaches at Jamama Hospital Nursing School, 1970.

Handwriting on the wall

"I want my friend again." Osman stood before the school librarian, checking out a book he'd already read. Mary Gehman looked up from classifying books. With the help of Rhoda Kennel, she had worked her way through 1500 books. Boys and books—her life. The monotony of hours spent at readying books for the shelves was broken by a pet monkey, a curious goat, a donkey's head thrust through the open door, and the campus dog. Books came from the United States Information Service, the American ambassador, Peace Corps neighbors, Books Abroad, and missionary staff members. Hundreds still boxed awaited shelving. "I like to work with books," Mary once wrote. "But to help the boy and the book to meet is much more rewarding." New books for a new library in a new school.

The dedication of the Shebelli Secondary School—February 18, 1972. "Welcome to our Distinguished Guests," the large bold banners assured the regional governor and other officials present. Their speeches said, "Education helps a poor nation conquer disease, ignorance, and poverty." Their accolades again praised the Mennonite Mission and the Somali teachers for their "superior educational program." All toured the 21 new classrooms, dormitories, and recreational center, funded by the Evangelical Churches of Germany and the Lancaster Mennonites of Pennsylvania. A facility for 200 students.

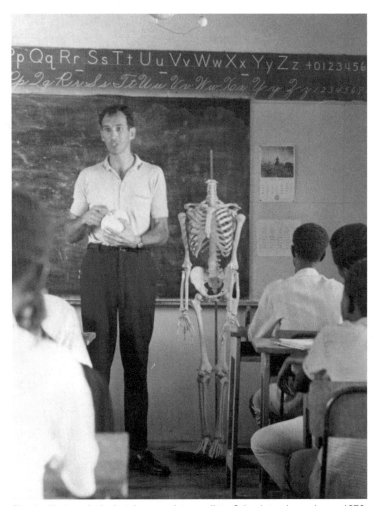

Chester Kurtz, principal at Jamama Intermediate School, teaches science, 1970.

Harold Reed, Major Warsame, President Major General Mohamed Siad Barre, and Ali Samatar. The Regional Governor cuts the ribbon to officially open the Shebelli Secondary School, Johar, February 18, 1972.

Shebelli Secondary School, Johar, 1972.

One other banner hung on the outside of the library boldly declared the nation's confident vision: "Scientific Socialism Turns Knowledge into Practical Reality." Were the words "a handwriting on the wall"? Would the slogan's acclaimed promises of a secular Eden be fulfilled? By the time Bertha Beachy again stood on the campus of the Shebelli Secondary School 20 years later, the desolate, bombed-out classrooms revealed the bitter fruit of that harvest.

The right to be Somali

"Somalia has a right to be itself," said Hershey Leaman, a breezy and efficient missions administrator at Salunga. "Furthermore, it has the right to determine how it will become itself. Obviously those alien influences which frustrate that goal must be curtailed. The Mennonite Mission, as guests in Somalia, respects their approach; indeed, we commit ourselves to cooperation." Why these words?

Revolution Day, October 21. Merchants shut up shop; government bureaucracies closed down; headmasters dismissed students. Everyone poured out into public areas to celebrate National Honor. Suddenly, a helicopter dropped out of the white morning skies over Mogadishu. As it chopped the air above the throngs of people, it threw down leaflets. Printed Somali words. Finally, after decades of dissension, Somalia's leaders in 1972 decided that their language should be written in a Latin script—not Arabic, not Osmanian. Somalis could now read Somali!

The euphoria of the morning's proclamation had not worn off when the government issued another by radio: "With immediate effect, all private schools are nationalized so that the government can more effectively convey Somali cultural values to Somali students through the use of written Somali."

David Shenk mused: "More than 30 missionary teachers collectively invested over 200 years—the home Mission Board,

1.5 million dollars." Ed and Jean Rissler observed with a wry spin: "Relieved of our institutions, we missionaries have become freer to live with people instead of administer programs." The missionaries felt that the nationalization of their schools was not a result of deteriorating relationships with Somalis. Yet, over the next two years all medical personnel, the agronomist, and a few teachers with degrees in religion were dismissed from the country. Buildings, facilities, and equipment now were the nation's. Without compensation.

Somali fish seller, Mogadishu.

A shepherd for the fellowships

Soon the last Mennonite Mission teachers would need to leave Somalia; the Mogadishu fellowship needed a leader. After many weeks of prayer and discernment, they gathered to affirm the one whom they believed God had called to be their teacher and shepherd.

Friday, July 18, 1975. "Upon this confession of faith and these promises which you have made before God and these witnesses, I herewith charge you . . . to instruct, comfort, and encourage the believers . . . to be a faithful shepherd of the flock of God."

Roy Brubaker, the last ordained Mennonite missionary in Somalia, quietly spoke those words. His hands lay on the head of kneeling Adam, a part-time lay teacher for the believers' group in Mogadishu. Twenty were present, witnessing this passing of leadership responsibility from North American missionary to Somali.

Adam, in response, quoted this text: "Jesus went around all the towns and villages announcing the good news of the kingdom. The people moved him to pity: they were like sheep without a shepherd." "I cannot do this work alone," Adam added. "I need God's help and the help of this group."

The very next morning, Adam was summoned to the Mogadishu Police Station. Officials wanted to know about the meeting, and what responsibilities his leadership would entail.

A week later, Roy, a teacher at a technical school in the capital, with his family, left the country. It seemed most fitting that the passing of this mantle should be from the gentle Roy Brubaker, himself a model of the Good Shepherd. His prayer for Adam on this occasion included, "Enrich him with good judgment, endow him with patience, keep him faithful until the Chief Shepherd appears."

Neil Reimer (seated at desk) and Jane Myers (Hooley), Somalia Mennonite Mission teachers at Somalia Institute of Public Administration (SIPA), with Interim Director Ahmed Musa Geddi (standing), and student Abdi, 1973.

'Services not needed'

Cornelius (Neil) Reimer, representative of the remaining Mennonites, sat across the desk from Suleyman Maxamud Adan, director general of the Ministry of Education.

Nine o'clock, April 28, 1976. First came the official words of appreciation for the decades of fine work by the Mennonite Mission teachers. Then: "With the graduation of 280 teachers from Lafoole College of Education, your services are not needed after May 7." The director then handed Neil the official notice to the same effect. *Jamhuuriyadda Dimog, Soomaaliya,* announced the letterhead in Somali. But the short text was written in English. Curiously, typed on the letter was: TOP SECRET. Top secret for whom? Within days every village and town on the 500-mile stretch of southern Somalia knew that the Revolutionary Council had terminated the contracts of all the Mennonite Mission teachers.

The teachers had ten days, but were given another thirteen to be out of the country. No Mennonite staff remained at Jamama, Kismayu, or Mahaddei. The government had assigned four to the secondary school at Johar; six Mennonites taught in the capital but lived scattered in rented facilities.

The scramble: notify the Somali friends; settle contracts with employees and landlords; sell, give away, or pack to ship personal effects; join the believers in one last fellowship; hold teas—and weep: one was leaving too abruptly the beautiful Somali people.

The believers found space in the Catholic cathedral for Friday worship. The last teachers checked into the Croce del Sud hotel. These last Mennonite missionaries spent their last night, May 19, 1976, where the Lind family had spent their first nights twenty-three years earlier, January 1953. The next morning it rained en route to the airport. Rain, always a whisper of promise in that dry and desolate land.

Croce del Sud Hotel, where the first missionaries stayed in 1953, and where the last missionaries stayed in 1976.

Mary Gehman with Salad, a student at Shebelli Secondary School, 1970.

Wedding of Said Samatar and Lydia Glick on the basketball court at the Somalia Mennonite Mission compound in Mogadiscio, June 10, 1970. David Shenk officiated. Standing from left to right: John Zook, Sureyan, Said Samatar, Lydia Glick, and Zeinab.

Annebelle Roth and daughters, Lisa and Christina, with school books, 1973.

Last letters

"To All My Beloved Brothers and Sisters in Christ of the Mennonite Mission in Mogadiscio, as of April 30, 1976:

"Beloved: The time we often wondered about coming has finally arrived. Even though we tried not to let it take us by surprise, it left me speechless. Still we must praise God with the same joy as if nothing happened at all. God has given us the joy of knowing each other. Praising him together and thanking him together. Now we must learn to thank him for moments that hurt us all deeply.

"Each one of you has served great purposes in this land. The most important being that you were instruments in establishing [a Christian fellowship in Somalia] . . . . I count myself a beneficiary of this wonderful deed of yours. Right now I cannot see anything other than sitting still and hoping in the Lord.

"In my meditation this afternoon, my heart rejoiced in singing hymn 326 in *The Mennonite Hymnal*: 'God is the refuge of his saints, When storms of sharp distress invade; Ere we can offer our complaints, Behold him present with his aid!'"

With love,
a Somali friend

"May 15, 1976

"To the President, Somali Democratic Republic:

"On behalf of the personnel of the Somalia Mennonite Mission and the Eastern Mennonite Board of Missions and Charities, I would like to thank you personally, and the people of Somalia, for the courtesies extended to us during our stay in Somalia. It has been our privilege to watch the progress of this nation over the 23-year period that we have been in Somalia. . . .

"On behalf of the Mission, we wish you success in carrying out the great responsibilities as Head of State. . . ."

Sincerely,
Neil Reimer

Velma Eshelman (Nzesi), nurse, with village women in Garissa, northeastern Kenya, 1975.

Now what

"What do we do with ten Somalia missionaries suddenly without a country?" Ken Nissley, associate director of overseas missions at Salunga, queried his board.

Within two months of leaving Somalia, Bertha Beachy pioneered a literacy project among the Somali and other language peoples of Kenya's Northeastern Province. The territory lay against Somalia, one of the three points not yet joined to the proud white star of the Republic of Somalia's national flag. Thirty miles from Nairobi the tarmac road ended, then began 150 of dust or mud. The team took extra food, water, and gas, in case their Land Rover broke down, a vehicle donated by the Christian Council. "Deep ruts made by heavy trucks were treacherous," Bertha reported. "High centers tore off mufflers. Once we wasted five days on that road!"

Also in Nairobi since their 1973 expulsion from Somalia were David and Grace Shenk, and Ron and Ruth Ann Hartzler (who had taught at Kismayu), now at work in Islamic ministries. One of their first projects included revising *The People of God*, a Bible correspondence study course for Muslims. Swahili and Somali translations and testings of the English text took another three years.

Also by September, the Ed and Jean Rissler family were living among the Somali, the Turkana, the Samburu, and the Boran, all nomadic peoples in the northern part of Kenya, also next door to Somalia. Ed long felt that he could fulfill a more basic need among Somalis if he taught agriculture rather than chemistry. There at the Garba Tula Secondary School set in a rocky desert, a bit of that vision was tested. In addition to math and science classes, he added an ag club: one group grew chickens, a second erected a small greenhouse for vegetables. Ed also joined community efforts at digging a well and building an earthen dam. Water!

Jane Myers (Hooley) transferred to teach in Sudan, Esther Becker to teach in Zambia; the remaining five Somali missionaries returned to North America.

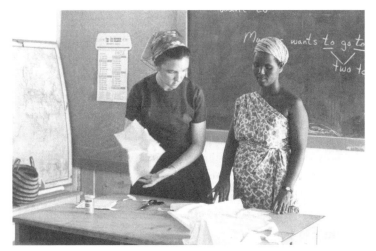

In Mahaddei, Elaine Good explains a sewing pattern to a Somali woman, 1972.

My experience with Mennonites

Ahmed Geddi Mohamud
Former Principal, Shebelli Secondary School

Early in 1965 I joined one of the Mennonite institutions as an unqualified teacher. When I graduated from Senior Secondary School, Sheikh, Somaliland, I was one of two students selected for a scholarship to France in the field of statistics. I came to Mogadishu full of hope. At the scholarship section of the Ministry of Education I introduced myself as the recipient of the scholarship. To my dismay I came to know that my position was taken away by a son of a Minister. Thus, I swallowed the bitter pill of nepotism and injustice in my early years.

To eke out my living I had to look for a job. A colleague also from Sheikh, I was told, was teaching at a Mission School in Mahaddei. He introduced me to Mr. David Shenk, principal of Shebelli Intermediate School, Johar. I was hired to teach math and officiate sports. Mohamud Togane (who soon left with a scholarship to the Unites States), Abdiraham Fao, and Sheikh Mohamed (on assignment from the Ministry of Education) were other Somali staff members.

There were two systems of education. The British 3, 4, 4, year system in the north of Somalia and the Italian 5, 3, 3, year system in the south. The Mennonite schools were the only institutions where English was the instructional medium. English was popular among the Italian-speaking Somali communities.

Parents who could afford the fees sent their kids to the Mission boarding schools. Adults came in droves to the Adult Learning Centers at Mogadishu and Kismayu.

Brought up in a boarding school environment throughout my own schooling, I enjoyed working at Shebelli School. Activities I admired and still recall include:

Flag Raising. Early after the morning tea, students assembled and stood on a designated number. Songs were recited. Announcements about the school's daily activities were made. It was an exuberant exercise.

Study Hall. It was an enforced privilege. Students were to study in the classrooms to do their evening assignments and projects. A Duty Teacher on site supervised the students.

Sports. The most important extracurricular activity that kept students on campus was sports. The expanding city of Johar completely surrounded the school compound. Thus, tug-of-war and soccer matches between staff and students were popular. For tug-of-war, with Chester Kurtz as our anchor, teachers were always the winners! The student soccer teams let the teachers win whenever they wanted a town-leave that evening!

The Mennonite Health Clinics of Mahaddei and Jamama were also valuable additions to the well-being of the ordinary masses. In October 1972 all private education institutions were nationalized (Egyptian, Catholic, and Mennonite schools). The

Mission staff was told to leave. Luckily and coincidentally, I was appointed the principal of the flourishing Shebelli Secondary School. Top people in the Ministry of Education and I convinced the new "soldier" minister to keep the Mission staff, otherwise the school would academically collapse.

In 1976 all religious agencies (the AZHAR, the Catholics, and the Mennonites) were expelled from the country because the so-called "socialist" government was not comfortable with their social and humanitarian programs. Contact between Somalis and foreigners, especially westerners, was discouraged. I was demoted and transferred to a remote region to head a school with only nine students in the eleventh grade—because of my association with the Mennonite Mission.

When the empty shell of "Scientific Socialism" cooled down, and I had become the director general in the Ministry of Education, we requested the Mennonite Mission to come back as individuals. They were based in major institutions: Curriculum Development Center, Women Education Center, Institute of Adult Education, and Technical Teacher Education College, until the civil war began in 1990. As education workers, the Mennonites left quite an impression in the hearts of many Somalis. They were people of compassion, who rendered significant services. They comfortably worked in devout Muslim communities who accepted them as social workers that had no hidden agenda.

Education was one of the first casualties in the Somali civil war, which continued unabated in many parts of Somalia. For over a decade the school-age children were without education. Unfortunately, thousands of youth were lured to join the many clan-based militias that were responsible for the destruction that took place in many parts of Somalia since 1991. When attempts were made to revive community education, the Mission rallied support for education. They believed that education was the springboard for promoting a culture of peace based on mutual respect. The SAACID "helping" School in Mogadishu and Amoud University are typical examples. Somalis want to commend Mennonites on their remarkable efforts to serve the younger generation and to renew their hope for the future.

Somalis are alone in the Horn of Africa. History has not been kind to this part of the region. More than a century ago through the scramble for the African continent, the Somali territory was divided up among the colonial powers (France, Britain, and Italy) and Ethiopia. The five points of the star in the Somali flag signify the ambitions of a greater Somalia. At independence in 1960 the British Protectorate (Somaliland) and the Italian-supervised UN trusteeship (Somalia) united to form the Somali Republic. Immediately Somalia forged links with the Soviet Union which provided technical and military support, while Ethiopia was an ally of the U.S., building one of the largest armies in sub-Saharan Africa.

The conflict that affected many parts of Somalia can be linked directly to the 1977 Ogaden war, a Cold War pawn. The superpowers switched sides to defeat a former ally. Defeat in the Ogaden war with Ethiopia supported by Russia, Cuba, and South Yemen led to the emergence of armed opposition in exile. The eventual overthrow of the Siad Barre government in 1991 and the ensuing collapse of the Somali State created intolerable humanitarian conditions.

International relief and security operations that followed in 1992 brought help to a needy population, but it failed to being an end to the inter-clan militia conflict. The fighting of 1991 triggered a massive exodus of people from Somalia, mainly of trained Somalis.

The Mennonite agencies participated in the humanitarian relief efforts to save lives in the mainland and in refugee camps in neighboring countries. In the same manner, the Mennonites familiar with the plight of Somalis have welcomed them to Canada and the Unites States and helped them to settle. CASOFA (Canadian Somali Friendship Association) formed in 1992, under the leadership of Victor and Viola Dorsch, helped Somali refugees coming to the greater Toronto area and the Waterloo region.

In a world changing fast around them, the Somalis are still in disarray. More than a dozen reconciliation conferences were held since 1993. Agreements were signed, but not honored. Somalia is still a theater of civil conflict, primarily initiated by the old elite with lust for power. "When elephants fight, it is the grass that suffers." Masses are suffering. Somalis are strong people. They endure calamities. They are yearning for social order. It is my hope that the upcoming reconciliation conference in Eldoret, Kenya, will rescue Somalis from living at the margins of human society. It should set the stage for the regeneration of local leadership that could rekindle the sentiments of nationalism, whereby Somalia could come together with amity and for co-existence.

Toronto, Canada
October 2002

Nineteen 80s

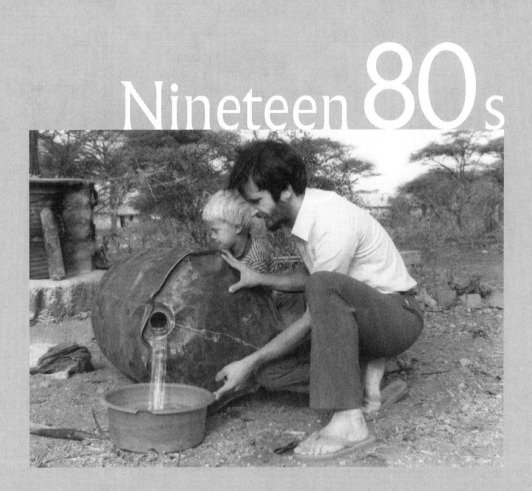

Refugees who received corn return to their homes in the camp, 1982. *Previous page:* Dean Brubaker with son, David, gets water from a drum at school in Rhamu, Kenya, 1984.

Years of refugees

If the 1960s were the "Golden Years" in Somalia, the 1980s were the "*Qaxooti* (Refugee) Years." Refugees, the result of stupid and bloody wars between nations, tribes, clans. Refugees, the hapless victims of a widespread, two-year drought followed by massive flooding. Refugees, too many to count, difficult even to estimate. In January 1980, the UN noted that Somalia had "375,000 refugees in camps and 650,000 in villages and towns." By June, *Time* magazine wrote, "The Horn of Africa has more than 1.7 million refugees from unresolved conflicts." Two years later, 37 refugee camps existed each with 15,000—20,000 people, some camps populated mostly by women and children. Many refugees, traditionally nomadic herdsmen who lived by means of camel and goat herds, had little experience raising maize and squash.

Somalia had encountered many problems during the 1970s. The Ogaden region straddling the ill-defined Somali-Ethiopian border was claimed by both nations. Skirmishes as early as the mid-60s erupted into open warfare throughout the 1970s, a war chiefly financed by Russia at first. The grand scheme of a Greater Somalia collapsed when Russia switched sides, backing a Marxist regime in Ethiopia on the successful coup d'etat against its aging emperor, Haile Selassie. Somalia was no longer a happy, confident land. The government became jittery and displayed the ugly characteristics of dictatorship, bitter at being abandoned. The Somalis could only turn again to the outside communities for help. Many died due to severe shortages; many nobly shared with each other. International agencies together with the Somali government inaugurated massive feeding and emergency medical programs.

When the rains failed, the tented populations of war-weary refugees swelled to accommodate victims of drought, famine, and disease. By UN estimates, "Somalia had more refugees per population than any other country in the world."

North American Mennonites again would hear the call to enter Somalia.

Janine Rands observes a Somali tailor, 1983.

Mennonites in Somalia: Act II

Ken Nissley, Isaq, and Ahmed Geddi, director of training and curriculum development, confer, 1982.

The question asked of Bert Lind two decades ago—"What is the Mennonite propaganda?"—was not asked on this second entry of Mennonites into Somalia.

Then an earnest young man had said, "I've been to the Russian embassy and the Chinese embassy and the American embassy and asked for their propaganda and received it. What is your propaganda?" But this time the Somalis knew: Mennonite missionaries were people of the Jesus Way with great empathy

for Somalis. They again welcomed the Mennonites. The first personnel in 1980 were with Mennonite Central Committee (MCC), "a Christian resource for meeting human need." Those volunteers bringing food, water, sanitation, medicine, and craft programs soon learned the high value of their denominational coinage in that Muslim country. Canadian MCC directors noted that their relief personnel benefitted greatly from the good legacy of the earlier Mennonite missionaries to Somalia, writing: "They generated great respect for Mennonite ministries."

Earlier that same year the UN commissioner for refugees to Somalia asked MCC to send twelve workers. "By our quick action in recruiting personnel and providing material aid, we are taken by the UN and the government as an agency on which they can count," stated Ray Brubacher, MCC Africa director.

The following year, 1981, the Somali government invited the Eastern Board to send at least four teachers for significant posts in Mogadishu. "This is a modern-day Macedonian call," said Hershey Leaman at Salunga. It seemed only fitting that the last couple to leave Somalia, Neil and Margaret Reimer, were among the first to return five years later. They transferred from an MCC assignment in Botswana. Fae Miller, a pioneer teacher/registered nurse to Somalia in the early 1950s, also volunteered to return as a teacher of nutrition. "I go with a little fear," she said, "but I also go with hope."

Corn for the Horn

"Awesome! Absolutely an awesome sight— bags upon bags of corn, 5,100 tons of corn!" Ardith Frey, an MCC representative, stood on the Mogadishu docks with her husband Marvin in January 1982, watching cranes piled with bags of corn unloading the Halcoussis anchored off shore. On the pier the bags were carried one-at-a-time on the backs of Somali workers—for five days and five nights—to empty the ship from Toledo, Ohio. From the Mogadishu port, CARE vehicles hauled the corn north to 27 refugee camps filled with Ogaden Somalis. "The corn in this shipment will feed camp populations for twenty-five days," Ardith reported. "Hundreds of thousand of Somalis displaced by war and famine welcome this food from generous Americans."

"A mountain of corn!" was the way Allen Kauffman, one trucker of the corn to Toledo, described the sight two months earlier, November 1981. He stood in the chilly air with over 250 people gathered for a dedicatory prayer. The Halcoussis arrived already carrying 3,000 tons of bulk corn gathered by Ontario Mennonites. The Great Lakes and East Coast regions of the Mennonite Disaster Service (MDS) organized the efforts in the States. Corn for the Horn poured out of America's Horn of Plenty: grain elevators dried corn without charge; volunteers bagged and trucked corn to the pier. From Toledo, the ship

Distribution of corn at refugee camp, 1982.

Women's leader Zeinab and MCC worker Lou Murray (Gorvett) outside home at Suriya Refugee Camp, 1982.

went up to Montreal where it took on another 3,000 tons of corn and 2,250 tons of wheat, peas, and lentils contributed by the Canadian government. These latter grains were dropped off at Assab, Ethiopia, for famine victims in that nation's region of the Ogaden. Churches also gave $400,000 to cover shipping fees and inland trucking costs in the Horn of Africa.

"Corn for the Horn," the *Missionary Messenger*, EMM's magazine, bore that corny title in August 1983, with a story about the delivery of the greatest shipment ever of material aid by North American Mennonites. MCC had chartered an entire cargo ship.

Water reservoir construction for refugee farm nursery, 1981.

Two women return

"I'd like to visit Merlin's grave," Dorothy Grove said. "It's something I've never done." When the Alitalia flight touched down at Mogadishu in 1985, a 23-year loop closed. "When I left Mogadishu in the summer of 1962, it seemed as though I had left half of myself behind. I was glad I could return to Somalia to get in touch with my past." Dorothy previously served in Somalia, 1960-1962, with her husband Merlin, who was killed by a citizen convinced that the Mennonite Mission schools were a threat to his faith. Now she returned to work as a nurse for five months with Families for Children, a Canadian agency that cared for 214 war orphans. "My greatest thrill was to be greeted by young men who knew Merlin as their teacher at Mahaddei," Dorothy wrote. Those months in Mogadishu ended too quickly. "When I left, I shed a few tears for Somalia and the Somalis I love. I took home with me new and renewed memories I shall cherish in years to come."

After a ten-year absence, Elizabeth Nissley also returned to Somalia. Earlier, with her husband Ken, she had spent seven years in Somalia. Now, with Ken, she came with two preteen daughters and two teenage sons. She needed "assurance that our family was not too large to send." She also needed assurance that returning at age forty "was not a midlife crisis, not nostalgia for a simpler lifestyle, not an escape from American

Elizabeth Nissley with Saida, course writer for Women's Education Department 1986.

values." Elizabeth's journal the year before leaving for Somalia notes the soul's battle to hear a clear calling. A nurse at first without an assignment, Elizabeth's hospitality became her mission, besides caring for her family. She lived Henri Nouwen's definition of spiritual hospitality—receptive to new experiences, different ideas, and strangers—as she served countless teas and meals to Somalis, colleagues, and international visitors—the stuff of practical hospitality. Later, EMM assigned Elizabeth to be co-mission leader with her husband, the Mogadishu believers chose her as an elder in their fellowship, and the Women's Education Center employed her as an instructor.

City courtyard vegetables

"Let's dig up the courtyard and plant vegetables," Ed Rissler suggested. "We must demonstrate that crops will grow." The site was the Curriculum Development Centre of the Ministry of Education, Mogadishu, 1985. Urban agriculture.

But Rissler's enthusiasm for growing things in Somalia was tempered by his six previous years of teaching at the Shebelli Secondary School, Johar. When, in the mid-1970s, classes had been suspended so students could fulfill the government edict to go into the bush to teach Somali literacy, Ed and Ken Nissley dug a canal from the Shebelli River to the campus. And while teaching biology and chemistry, Ed had "slowly involved students in more practical studies: gardening, poultry keeping, and animal husbandry." The tiny experimental garden grew to five acres; five hens became 120; 80 students helped to "farm"; 20 to raise lambs and kid goats. Then, suddenly it was over. "In April 1976 we were told to go home," Ed noted. "Now, nine years later (1985) the same government, the same people, asked for us to return."

When the Ed and Jean Rissler family returned to Somalia, this time to Mogadishu, Ed was given supervision of preparing booklets for Somali farmers. His colleagues at the Centre—Abdullahi Ahmed Hussein and Abdulkaadir Hasan Ahmed—translated from English into Somali. Others drew pictures and diagrams to accompany the text.

Ed Rissler discusses layout details with Somali graphic artists for Cilmiga Deganka (environmental textbooks) at the Curiculum Development Center, 1987.

Ed Rissler was only one of a dozen teachers offered by the Mennonite Mission to Somalia through the 1980s. A diverse set, they came from Pennsylvania and Indiana, Maryland and Virginia, Ohio and Minnesota, Canada and the Netherlands. The Somali government placed most of them at its National Technical Teacher Education College. By July 1986, the Ministry of Foreign Affairs again approved the registration of Mennonite Missions to operate programs. Daniel and Jan Gerber went to Kismayu; Lamar and Barbara Witmer to Merka.

Kenyan Somalis

"Aren't you here to convert Muslims to Christianity?" This first question caught Don Yoder completely by surprise that morning in 1986. "If not, why have you come to Eastleigh?" The Mennonite missionary and a leader of the Young Muslim Association sat in the "dialogue room" at Eastleigh Fellowship Centre. They first met at an Islamic Seminar hosted by Mennonite agencies in Nairobi, Kenya. "This is the first of five questions," the young man said. With paper and pen in hand, he settled down to take notes on their three-hour dialogue.

Eastleigh is a densely populated, semi-slum area of Nairobi, home to Somali, Ethiopian, and Sudanese refugees. The government acknowledges the area to be "a breeding ground for crime; guns, drugs, forgery, and prostitution are rampant." In this 20-block, 20,000-person arena, Mennonites with a vision dedicated their community center on June 1980. After cutting the ribbon and unveiling the plaque, Ahmed Abdallah, director general of the Supreme Council of Kenya Muslims, said, "It's not enough for Christians to read books written by Christians about Islam, and vice versa. Dialogue takes place only when we sit down face-to-face."

Between 300 and 500 people weekly passed through Eastleigh Center: women for sewing classes, students for the library and a quiet place to study, adults for evening English and literacy classes, anyone for educational films, the Nairobi Mennonite congregation for worship and Sunday school. In one office a Somali woman supervised the day-to-day work for the *People of God* Bible correspondence course, first begun in Johar by David Shenk. Today the Centre also coaches the "Mennonite Knights," a basketball team that rose to the top in Kenya's semi-professional league. And always the inquirers come with their questions about the Christian faith. "Everyone in Eastleigh is welcomed here," said Em Yoder, "for tea and talk."

Students study at Eastleigh Fellowship Centre, Nairobi, Kenya, 1983.

A far frontier

That March (1986) Nancy Brubaker thought her drinking water tasted of camel urine.

The Daua River had dried up a month ago. Somalis dug holes in the riverbed to scoop out water. Many were sick with dysentery. The temperature was 120 in the shade. For two-and-a-half years, no measurable rain fell on Rhamu. Nancy walked nowhere without encountering scores of dead cows, goats, even camels. Each morning Somali herdsmen lifted their surviving cattle to their feet.

"These people are worshipers of Allah," Nancy observed. "They say that everything is written and cannot be escaped. Whatever happens to them is the will of Allah. They do not presume to argue with Allah. What is written is written."

Six hundred air miles beyond Nairobi, Rhamu lies in the semiarid region of Kenya's Northeast Province. Soldiers in khaki guard the border against Somalis and Ethiopians. But Somali nomads with their camels roamed that three-corner territory for a thousand years, indifferent to political demarcations of the nineteenth or twentieth centuries. "As long as thorn scrub grows to support goats and camels, the land is not a desert," insisted Dean Brubaker, Nancy's husband. "It's only semiarid. About 5,000 people live in Rhamu, 15,000 at Mandera, 40 miles down river." In these towns Ken and Judy Nafziger and Lois Ranck (Hicks) taught and did medical work.

At Rhamu Secondary School, Dean taught math to 120 boys, many the sons of nomadic fathers who still followed their herds in search of pasture. Nancy, mother of three small sons, moved among the Somali women who took her in. She enjoyed their hospitality, cooked their local foods—*injera* and camel roast—and learned respect for their simple life. "Women of Rhamu lived happily with few demands on the earth's limited resources. They did not strive for privacy and independence. From their little they shared generously."

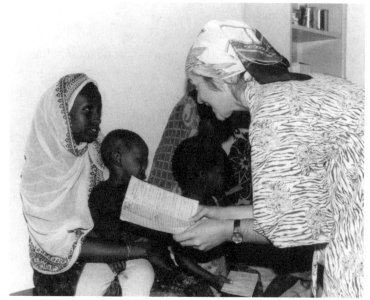

Lois Ranck (Hicks) in clinic at Rhamu, Kenya, 1986.

Under Five Clinic

Medina had three strikes against her: a girl, an orphan, with a handicap. When the doctor diagnosed Medina's condition as cerebral palsy, her mother left her infant daughter at a Mogadishu hospital and never came back.

"I wanted to be in touch with the suffering people in my area," Mary Bradshaw said. "Teaching at the Women and Children's Hospital put me in touch with the 'Under Five Nutrition Clinic.' I gave basic preventive health lessons to the mothers who stayed with their sick children in the pediatrics wards." Then Mary met tiny abandoned Medina, who lay all day in her crib and sometimes got a little milk from a cleaning woman.

"Asking questions, I found one woman who agreed to care for her if first I took Medina home for one month until her health improved." Thus, in 1987, the Bradshaw family entered Medina's world and she into theirs. "Somehow, the presence of her frail, vulnerable body in our living room assured us of the presence of God who had also entered our lives in a frail, vulnerable body," wrote Bruce Bradshaw. "She, too, was the image of God. She came to bless our lives."

"I saw my role as a presence to share these Somali mothers' pain," Mary said, "to listen to their concerns, to hold their starving babies, to absorb their sorrow. I did not want to be detached from their experience; I wanted to face it with them."

Through caring for Medina, Mary learned compassion for the mothers who came to the clinic with underweight babies. Those mothers were often pregnant again and had little time in their busy schedules to care for a sick child.

The Bradshaws lived in Mogadishu; Bruce taught business and economics at the National Technical Teachers Education College. They were another two of the dozen Mennonite Mission teachers in Somalia during the 1980s.

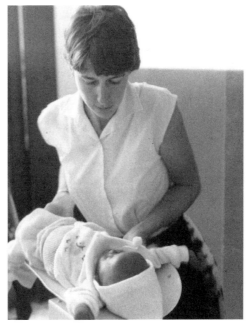

Mary Bradshaw at "Under 5 Nutrition Clinic" in Mogadishu, 1987.

Good news: a tinge of green

Ibrahim wanted to return to Ethiopia on the next repatriation convoy, but he still owed MCC 6,000 shillings (U.S. $15) on his Bluebird Zig-Zag Deluxe treadle sewing machine. But no one in the family had money. "I'm a God-fearing man," he told MCC worker Scott Coverdale, "I won't steal it." Coverdale told a story. He retold in Somali idiom one of Jesus' parables: "Once there was a rich chief who had herdsmen. One owed him 50 camels. . . but the chief had mercy on him and forgave his debt. Then that herdsman went to a friend who owed him a packet of tea. . . . Jesus said if God forgives our terrible sins, we should forgive each other. So, [Ibrahim], it's easy to cancel your little debt on the sewing machine." The grateful refugee said, "Jesus spoke the very truth." Coverdale gave Ibrahim a 10,000-yard roll of red thread and wished him Godspeed. "As I walked home," Coverdale wrote, "I prayed for the soil on which the seed fell today."

In 1987, while most of the Mennonite family taught in Mogadishu or worked in Merca, six MCC workers stayed by their programs in refugee camps. Theirs was the tenuous but arduous task of easing dependency on free food to producing food themselves. And that among people who were only temporary residents in a camp, with a climate inhospitable to crop-growing. Another of Coverdale's projects: helping to organize 50 Somali farmers into *Beerta Towfiq*, the Unity Farm cooperative. The experts "advised me to steer clear of anything like a cooperative" with these Somalis and refugees. Yet, months later the joyful shouts of farmers rose when the motor of the oily new irrigation pump started up and water flowed to their hand-dug farm plots. A week later, Coverdale walked to the farm, little dust clouds rising about his feet. "I heard the thrumming of the irrigation pump and the chanting of working farmers. As I looked across their fields, I believe I saw a tinge of green."

Scott Coverdale, MCC worker, chats with Muslim sheiks in Eastleigh, Nairobi, Kenya, 1984.

Bulletins from the front

Somalia, 1989.

January, Mogadishu. Somalia's decade-long military attempts to occupy Ethiopia's Ogaden area, home to an ethnic Somali majority, climaxed in a loss that undermined Somalia's government under dictator Siad Barre. He played subclan against subclan in attempts to stay in power.

February, Hargeisa. General Said Herzi Morgan, an army commander and son-in-law of President Barre, led a ruthless military campaign to put down a rebellion in Hargeisa, Northern Somalia, hiring Zimbabwean mercenary pilots, who destroyed 80 percent of that city's buildings.

March, Djibouti. Mike and Cindy Brislen, EMBMC teacher and nurse, continued their study of the French language in Strasbourg, France, in preparation for their assignment in Djibouti, home of many French-speaking Somalis and Afars.

April, Nairobi. *People of God*, a Bible correspondence course prepared for Muslims a decade ago by former Somali missionaries, reported translations into a dozen African and Asian languages. East Africa alone had nearly 6,000 Muslims enrolled in at least one of the four-booklet series.

Gerald Hiestand works with a Somali, 1981.

May, Mogadishu. Eastern Board sent Kevin and Sharon Yoder to teach at the Adult Education Center as an agriculturalist and at the Women's Education Institute as a nutritionist, their second three-year term in Somalia.

July, Mogadishu. Assassins murdered the Italian Catholic bishop in his cathedral, in which a handful of believers met for worship.

September, Akron, Pa., United States. Due to the escalating civil war, and with the second theft of an MCC Land Cruiser at gunpoint and rough-up of its personnel, MCC withdrew its final six workers from refugee camps.

Poor Somalia...

Said Samatar

Professor of African History
Rutgers University, NJ

"Poor Somalia, so far from Allah, and so close to the United States." I am, of course, paraphrasing that Mexican dictator of decades ago who said: "Poor Mexico—so far from God and so near to the United States."

I spoke those words in 1993, with the American military force sitting in my country, Somalia. Originally President Bush (Sr.) dispatched his men to join a United Nations humanitarian peacekeeping mission to protect the free distribution of foodstuffs to tens of thousands of refugees in the interior. The principle source of disorder centered in Mogadishu, the capital divided between clan warlords. U.S. forces then launched an intensive manhunt to arrest these leaders, but they united to fight back. Later, both the U.S. and the UN abandoned Somalia.

Fragmentation has long been a Somali characteristic. My people are individualistic and form coalitions as the need arises. It has been said, "In Somalia everyone is a sultan." The clan system both links and divides my people. Often subclans are bitterly divided against each other. One Somali saying goes: "I and my clan against the world. I and my brother against my clan." Nevertheless, Somalia must be saved. In that context, I often set out the following outline for peace:

First, revive the institution of elders. The current malaise stems from a moral vacuum. The present disaster is directly traceable to a tragic mismatch between moral authority possessed by the elders and senior notables of the clans, and physical coercive authority usurped by self-made warlords. To restore political and moral equilibrium, it is necessary to re-empower the elders.

Next, establish a neutral radio station for relaying information. Somalis trade in news and hearsay like Americans trade on the stock market and Arabs trade in petrodollars. Then assemble all the Somali poets to begin promoting peace through the radio station. People listen to poets. Poetry is how we ask the abiding questions—how are we, where did we come from, where are we going.

Third, initiate a program to gather the educated Somalis and make it safe for them to return to their homeland. Nearly 90 percent of Somalis with college education live abroad, in Canada, the U.S., Europe, and several African and Arab capitals. Much of the country has been left to the mercies of warlords, merchants, pastoralists, and the illiterate.

Next, establish a national police force to disband the militias. Any respectful treatment of warlords is astonishingly wrong-headed. They have no credibility among rank-and-file Somalis. It is their fighting and looting which brought famine to the breadbasket of Somalia. The very term is incorrect. "Warlord" implies a leader with disciplined followers. But Somali warlords command only as long as they lead their thugs to booty. Otherwise the "troops" will desert. For this reason, the warlords have no interest in peace. They do not have the power to make peace, only the power to make war.

I am not naive. I readily admit that these suggestions offer no absolute promise. These steps may not guarantee immediate peace, but they are steps toward sanity.

In addition to these points, I fear the rise of militant Muslim fundamentalists. Just as the conflict between constitutional and communist governments dominated this century, rivalry between Western humanist values and angry Muslim fundamentalists will dominate the next decades.

A decade later, as I review these points of my 1993 vision for peace, I feel more strongly than ever that my voice joined to other peacemaking schemes could still contribute to laying the base for lasting peace and reconstruction in Somalia.

September 2002

Refugee women at a camp in Somalia, with corn from an MCC shipment, 1982.

Somalia: a part of my heritage

Grant Rissler

Several years ago, while working for the Mennonite Central Committee's United Nations Office in New York City, I was privileged to help set up several advocacy meetings with UN officials for Bertha Beachy, recently returned from her final term working with the Somali people, and Fatima Jibrell, managing director of Horn Relief Organization, one of Bertha's many Somali friends and colleagues.

Throughout the two days of meetings, I felt incredibly blessed to welcome Bertha and Fatima to New York, and to arrange opportunities for them to share their expertise on Somalia with the United Nations community. Partly, the blessing was being able finally to give something, however small, back to the country that filled two years of my childhood. But also, the blessing was in the rare opportunity to give back across the generations of work in Somalia: to welcome an elder who, a quarter century before, had welcomed my parents, fresh from college, into EMM's work in Somalia.

Those of us who joined the Mennonite journey in Somalia as wide-eyed children sticking close to our parents' sides lack the memories of students who learned and blossomed in Johar, or buildings that gradually took form and substance, focuses instead more so on how those years changed us.

Looking back, at the age of 25, on the years I lived in a white-washed cinder block house just off the Kilometer 5 traffic circle in Mogadishu, I often wonder what would be different now, had my parents not accepted that second call to Somalia in 1985. Who would I be? Who would I be without the memories of Halley's comet streaking over the Indian Ocean, without the games of tag on concrete courtyards so hot we hopped from one bare foot to the other just to stand still?

The answers come rarely as certainties, and most in the form of doubts. I doubt I would be in a master's program in International Relations. I doubt I would have spent two-and-a-half years in Mennonite Voluntary Service after college. I doubt I would have as strong a defense against the elements of consumerism and instant gratification that twist through the North American culture of which, willing or not, I am a part. I doubt my faith would be as strong, or as flexible, as it has grown in the last 15 years since I last saw Somalia.

There is at least one certainty, however: the certainty that Somalia, and the believers, friends and colleagues I half remember, still hold sway in the paths I choose to walk, the questions I am impelled to ask about peace, justice, and faith, and the openness I try to hold, listening for the call of God in midst of each day's journey. To do otherwise would be to betray a heritage.

Bologna, Italy
September 2002

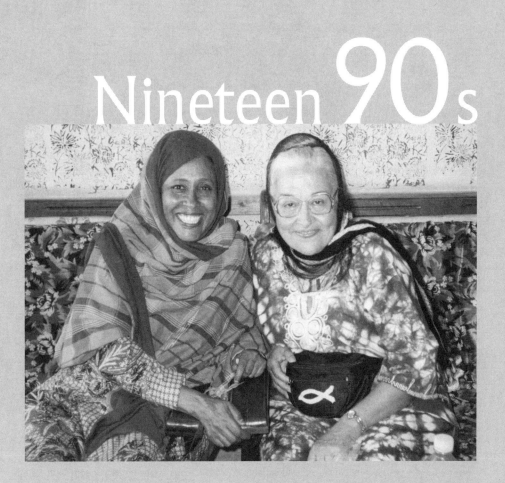

Bonnie Bergey with Somali women in Mogadishu, 1992. *Previous page:* Bertha Beachy with Fatima Jibrell, director of Horn of Africa Relief, 1998.

Decade begins with a woman

She thought, "So, this is where my life ends—I'll die in this black and green dress." Early in 1992 Bonnie Bergey huddled with other passengers on the back seat of a car in a Somali town. Armed bandits flagged the car and stuck their guns through the windows. It had happened before—militant outlaws of clans stole private vehicles at gunpoint. Only a year before, armed youth had taken an MCC vehicle. Here now, a bandit threw the driver of Bonnie's car from the seat and climbed behind the wheel. When he could not start the car, a gun battle ensued between townspeople and the armed robbers. Through negotiations with the bandits, the townspeople won. After the militants stormed off, the townspeople, embarrassed that a robbery had been attempted in their town, gathered in the streets to sing and clap their visitors along on their journey. "*Alxamdullila*!" (God be praised) they cried.

A Mennonite woman, Bonnie Bergey, was present in Somalia for the opening of the new decade—the 1990s. A Mennonite woman, Bertha Beachy, living in Nairobi, closed the decade.

From Mogadishu and Nairobi, Bonnie looked across five years of violent national events in Somalia and the tragedy engulfing the fractured lives of its peoples. She arrived in March 1990 as another Eastern Board-sponsored English instructor at the Teachers' Training College. Five years later, when she left East Africa, Bonnie was the Somali representative for EMBMC and MCC. Arriving in Mogadishu, Bonnie joined a professional Mennonite team which would grow to nine: a doctor, nurses, and teachers. They no longer lived together as families on a campus; the Somali government had nationalized those quarters almost two decades ago.

None of these Mennonite missionaries were naive; all were well aware of the possibility of the civil war escalating as tension mounted between the old dictator and clan leaders fast arming their people against President Barre. Mennonite team leader Kevin Yoder, in contact with government officials, "sensed their deep despair and near paralysis with the lack of fuel and funds." Armed groups of men began to roam Mogadishu's streets, looting markets, shops, homes. Still the Mennonite family, which lived apart at several locations about the capital, thought they could go quietly about their ministries. But by December 2, 1990, with whining bullets and artillery pounding day and night in the streets, the staff decided to leave Mogadishu temporarily for Nairobi. By the end of that month, forces loyal to President Barre and those that opposed him, the United Somali Congress, battled openly for Mogadishu. None of that EMBMC team returned to Somalia—except Bonnie, later.

The Eastern Board wanted to remain near Somalia, to keep a presence among the thousands of refugees streaming into Kenya, and to aid the believers in Mogadishu. "I wanted to stay," Bonnie said. The Board assigned her to the Mennonite

Office in Nairobi. Over the next four years, she made 15 trips back into Somalia.

In August 1991, Bonnie returned to Hargeisa with MCC representatives concerned with food and peace. She stood in rubble-filled streets before roofless houses with gaping ten-foot holes—the work of "armed anarchy." A year later on one trip, Bonnie officially closed down the rented Mennonite houses in Mogadishu and gave severance pay to the watchmen. She also arranged for the first of two EMBMC nurses to arrive during a cessation of the fighting. In 1993, an MCC Canada representative and Bonnie attended the opening session of a meeting of 300 clan elders to discuss peace. The Mennonites brought a $10,000 gift to the gathering, a sum that covered 10 percent of the months-long meeting expenses. Always of particular concern to Bonnie was aid to women's groups working at peace. On leaving Nairobi in June 1995, she mused, "I don't know what to do with my anger toward those Somali men who make a game of war at the expense of women and children."

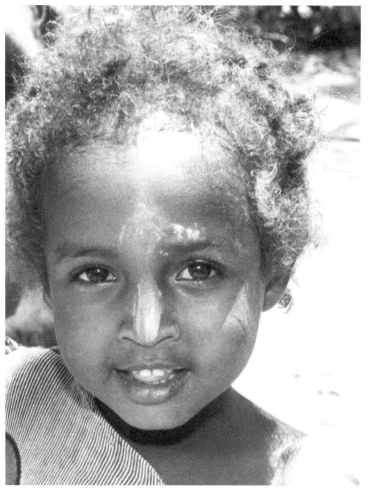

Somali child, 1994.

Civil war

Two dozen Somali believers slipped through a back door into a Catholic cathedral.
For some time now, they had gathered privately there for fellowship. That last Friday morning of December 1990, a man full of premonition took notes on the meeting. As he looked around, he noted the absence of the Mennonites. "We really miss our friends from the Mennonite Mission," he wrote. "Their participation was a clear display of God's unfailing love. Unfortunately, deteriorating security compelled them to leave Somalia last month." He later entitled his notes: "The Last Somali Fellowship Before the Civil War."

The next month, January 1991, looters burned the cathedral, the only remaining visible symbol of a Christian presence in the nation. The Catholic priest in charge, along with 60 others, came to the cathedral, thinking there they'd be safe. But government soldiers demanded keys to vehicles in the courtyard. Men, women, and children stormed in, smashed windows, and began to loot. "They even carried off cases of Eucharist wine," the Italian priest said. From a building next door, he watched as flames engulfed his cathedral. In the end, only the fire-blackened stone walls remained.

Outside, bodies littered the Mogadishu streets. The heavy artillery blasts by clan-based militia rattled the shuttered city. Pandemonium spread among Mogadishu residents. Clinics filled

Bertha Beachy revisits the Maternity/Child Care Clinic, Mahaddei, with a Somali delegation in 1996. The clinic was built by John Zook in the early 70s.

with the bloodied victims. At the fortified American embassy, hundreds of expatriates reenacted the Fall of Saigon. Helicopters lifted them out to a U.S. aircraft carrier in the Indian Ocean. Others got through the battle lines to chartered aircraft standing by at the airport secured by American troops, stationed there by U.S. President Bush (Sr.).

"Banditry, rebellion, and a breakdown of law and order put life at risk," reported the Associated Press. "Another African state lurched into anarchy last week," wrote *Time* magazine (l/14/91). Over several years, groups of Somali rebel armies undercut President Siad Barre's despotic regime. Then, early in 1991 these armies "closed in on the capital and smashed the government's rule," *Time* observed. Having disposed of Barre, the victorious rebel armies then turned their guns on each other. Subclans fought subclans as their leaders struggled for power.

Meanwhile, in the interior west of Mogadishu, a horrific famine was occurring. The UN mounted a 29-nation, 21-thousand military force in an attempt to insure the peaceful distribution of foodstuffs. Warehouses filled with imported emergency food needed 24-hour guarding. The port-of-entry for the relief materials needed guarding. Convoys carrying food to the interior needed guarding. Still, rebels overpowered guarded warehouses. Such action was dubbed "spontaneous distribution." Marguerite Michales of the *Globe and Mail* (4/20/93) declared that CARE steered its food directly to the warlord's warehouse. "They figured 50 percent was distributed to people who need it; 50 percent was diverted" to warlords.

"Armed anarchy" reigned as Somalia continued to spiral downward during the next 18 months. Then in June 1993, warlord Mohamed Aideed's thugs ambushed and killed 24 UN Pakistani peacekeepers. American military leaders concocted the idea of abducting Aideed's two top lieutenants to break the backbone of his lawless reign. Late afternoon, October 3, U.S. Army Rangers and Delta Force operators dropped from helicopters into a teeming Sunday market in the heart of Mogadishu. It's "a one-hour" operation, their officers declared. Instead, the Somalis shot down two high-tech Black Hawk helicopters. Thousands of heavily armed Somalis pinned down the 90 Americans for a terrible night of street fighting. In the morning 18 Americans and hundreds of Somalis lay dead. President Bill Clinton withdrew the American troops. Soon, the UN also abandoned Somalia.

Meanwhile in the States, Mennonites debated the propriety of Christian pacifists employing armed guards to accompany trucks loaded with relief food.

Military escorts

In November (1992), a number of humanitarian organizations and Christian agencies, including Church World Service and World Vision, called for "appropriately armed UN security forces tasked with protecting emergency supplies and staff." Although no longer present in Somalia, MCC declined to sign the request, even as Somalis lay dying. Some Mennonites of North America learned again (after Vietnam and Yugoslavia) that feeding the hungry could tangle with their pacifist theology. Uneasiness, unhappiness, and disagreement came in and sat down heavily in the Mennonite House for Peace. Should the church stay pure, compromise, or admit to a bipolar dualism?

Mennonite theologians carried on a debate in the 1993 winter and spring issues of the *Gospel Herald* (one of the parents of the contemporary *The Mennonite*).

J. R. Burkholder and Ted Koontz wrote (1/12/93): "We recognize that Mennonites today often disagree on the appropriate way for the church to respond to military actions of governments. Perhaps it is time to think again about some kind of dualism. By this we would acknowledge the importance of restoring order and accept the apparent need for governments sometimes to act with force or the threat of

Somali refugee children, 1993.

force. But we believe that as pacifist Christians, military action is not our calling. For Mennonites, this may be a time for silence. It may be a time to neither condemn nor advocate this particular use of military force."

J. Lawrence Burkholder wrote (3/16/93): "Somalia has placed Mennonites in a difficult position, and our theological response is indeed messy. With Somalia, we are caught, no matter what we do. Even if we do nothing, we are still morally culpable. It is ironical that while ambiguity is rooted in natural complexity and human sinfulness, love itself may drive God's people into ambiguous situations. The experience of ambiguity is the dark side of responsible love. Our theological conceptualization is more for our own satisfaction than as a serious response to Somalia. If Lancaster or Elkhart were in chaos because our government disintegrated, my guess is it would not take us long to develop a 'theology of order,' relying on Romans 13:1-7. The most humble and effective approach to peacemaking is to consider it incidental to more traditional relief and mission endeavors. The less premeditated, self-conscious, and specialized the better."

J. Denny Weaver wrote (4/27/93): "We must continue to reject 'just war' thinking. The most seductive of all American myths—guns and violence solve problems, provide security, and produce freedom—has tempted Mennonites as a peace church. With the absence of an overt military objective in Somalia, the supposedly humanitarian use of the army is more subtle and perhaps more dangerous to Mennonites. Some claim that the use of the U.S. Army to force the warlords into a cease fire creates more good than not using the army. If Mennonites are principled pacifists, they shouldn't fall into the use of justifiable war criteria to rationalize military action. Accepting an initial compromise to make limited use of a military presence is the beginning of a series of compromises, each one allowing yet more violence."

Meanwhile, MCC appointee Steve Elzinga was in Somalia on a ten-week "listening ear" assignment. "One should use a military escort only as a last resort—and after sufficient personal agony," he agreed. "But when the time came, I didn't struggle at all. The needs were so great, so many, so vast. I rode with the military."

And John Paul Lederach, on the staff of MCC's International Conciliation Service, wrote: "Negotiating with those who control guns is crucial so food can be delivered immediately. But a comprehensive, creative strategy for peace in Somalia must address much more than food and the way to deliver it to the people."

Ergada Wadatashiga Somaliyeed

General Mohamed Farah Aideed arrived at his office amid a flurry of jeeps, soldiers, and rifles. His military escort completed the security of a place already bristling with weapons: machine guns, rocket launchers, grenade launchers, 30 mm anti-tank guns. Wearing his trademark Muslim rimless cap and his ready smile, he extended a friendly hand to his guest.

John Paul Lederach, with armed escort, had arrived earlier. Now he shook hands with one of the two Mogadishu warlords vying for national power. August 1991 found Lederach of MCC's International Conciliation Service on a visit to the Horn: Djibouti, Somaliland (the former British territory that seceded from the Republic of Somalia), and Somalia. He was on a mission to meet with political and military leaders, even warlords, to explain the vision of the Somalia Peace and Consultation Committee (*Ergada Wadatashiga Somaliyeed*). Since 1989, Lederach had worked with Somalis to create a regular forum for dialogue across clan lines. *Ergada* then seemed one of the most imaginative schemes for reconciliation. Yet, to Lederach, Aideed seemed more interested in laying out military strategies than in plans for meeting urgent humanitarian needs. The general showed little interest in *Ergada*'s earlier meeting in Djibouti, which published accords.

Khadja Ali Osoble and Bertha Beachy at Eastern Mennonite University, 1998.

If Aideed in Mogadishu was disinterested about *Ergada*, the Chairman of the Central Committee in Hargeisa, Somaliland, was severely blunt. Ibrahim Meygag Samatar lectured Lederach: "*Ergada* is made up of people who did not engage in the fight in the hard years. It is unintelligible why people who refused to take part in the tough struggle now call us to an armchair discussion of reconciliation. A meeting of intellectuals is only self-serving. We invite them to come back and work with their people and put their fingers in the dirt. Otherwise, they can stay in their comfortable university chairs." Such responses showed how daunting and complex the work for Lederach and other peacemakers, how wide the gap between Somali clan leaders.

This was neither Lederach's first nor last tour of Somali states, or audience with government and military leaders, as he probed for ways to make heard his Mennonite people's voice joined with others. In October 1991, Lederach was invited to the Seychelles to participate in a major consultation of UN personnel with Somalis. Early 1993 found him in Addis Ababa, Ethiopia, where fourteen leaders of Somalia's warring clans met. Lederach did not participate in the formal UN-sponsored meetings. Rather, he joined the "corridor facilitators." These people arranged for talks between Somalis present but excluded from the formal UN discussions: traditional clan elders, women, poets, and others. August that same year,

Lederach along with Bonnie Bergey attended the opening session of the five-month gathering of 300 clan elders at Boroma, Somaliland. (It was to this conference MCC contributed $10,000 toward expenses.) Lederach identified two reasons for the meeting's success: "a series of local clan meetings preceded it, and clan elders initiated and conducted the meetings. When elders at local meetings negotiate solutions to local problems, then it is possible to build from local to regional meetings."

In several published articles and radio and television interviews, Lederach reiterated his convictions of what it would take for "a sustainable peace in Somalia." He said, "The urgency we feel in regards to food should not be used as leverage to push for a high-profile, internationally convened peace conference of select Somalis. Sustainable reconciliation in the Somali context must work from a regional strategy of sub-clan and inter-clan consultations building toward a national level forum. Also, we must do much more in support of intellectuals, elders, women, and poets who have initiated efforts for cross-clan dialogues."

Djibouti: 'Presence ministry'

In the late 1970s, with growing opposition from the Marxist government in Mogadishu, Somalia, Eastern Board looked for new ways to work with the Somali people. With encouragement from the Mennonite churches of East Africa, the Board considered Djibouti a logical place to expand their work in the Horn of Africa. The first exploratory visit by an EMBMC official occurred in 1980. A second visit in 1982 included a representative of the French Mennonite churches.

Djibouti lies in the northeastern corner of the Horn of Africa at the mouth of the Red Sea, across which lie Yemen and Saudi Arabia. It shares borders with Ethiopia and Somalia and enjoys extreme landscapes for a country the size of Massachusetts: juniper-forested rugged mountains, desert plateaus, volcanic moonscapes, salty Lake Assal at 450 feet below sea level. And Djibouti sweats with 110 degree heat in the port city.

Djibouti was colonized by the French more than 100 years ago and achieved independence in 1977, retaining a large French business and military community. It declared French the official language to blend the Afars of the North and the Somalis of the South, peoples joined by geography, history, and Islam.

After ten years of visits, prayers, and negotiations with the Djiboutian Ministry of Education, the first of EMBMC's secondary English teachers arrived. In January 1990, the Mike and Cindy Brislen family and veteran teacher Marian Hostetler began their assignments. Six months later, the Dean and Sandy Larimer family joined the Mennonite team. A third couple, Doug and Elaine Shenk, began similar teaching assignments in 1993.

Eastern Mennonite Missions' work in Djibouti is often called a "presence ministry." Susan Godshall, the Director for Africa, defines the mission as, "to serve Djiboutian society, in partnership with the Djiboutian government, while maintaining a Christian presence and giving an opportunity for dialogue with the Christian faith."

Further, Godshall declares, "The Anabaptist tradition . . . of tolerance and nonviolence, spoken by a servant community with an understanding of persecution, and presented from a position of powerlessness, has much to say in an Islamic country whose religious ancestors experienced the bloody Christian Crusades." (Brutal ventures in the eleventh, twelfth, and thirteenth centuries to forcefully win the Holy Land from Muslims.)

Marian Hostetler found Djiboutian women, though 90 percent illiterate, to be enterprising business people. Outside her school, 30 to 50 women daily set up tiny shops. "They bring their shops with them in wheelbarrows, shopping carts, or old baby carriages," she said. They sold cold drinks, cakes, watches; some with treadle machines sewed up a shift while the customer waited. Half of Hostetler's students were girls studying English. "What lies ahead for these young women?" she wondered.

Mark and Chantal Logan arrived in Djibouti July 1995, he to be mission director, she, from France, to teach French. Five years later they would be appointed representatives of EMM and MCC's missions to the Somali peoples.

Somali peacemaker wounded

He prayed, "God, please let me see my family before I die." January 12, 1992, Ahmed Haile woke from lost consciousness to find a friend, a nurse's aide, at a makeshift hospital amputating his leg without anesthesia. He watched the medic wrapping up for disposal his amputated lower leg, bone-shattered and still wearing his sock. Through the fog of pain, Haile had the presence of mind to call to his nephew, "Wait, there's money in my sock." He had hidden $315 in the sock of his right foot. "It's all I've got for this trip," he said.

Haile's trip to Mogadishu, sponsored by *Ergada*, began October 1991. He responded to an urgent call from members of his sub-clan, the Hawiye. Both key antagonists—interim President Ali Mahdi and General Mohamed Aideed—also belonged to the Hawiye clan. Centuries-old customary laws called for Haile's sub-clan to settle disputes within the Hawiye. In addition, Haile holds graduate degrees in peace studies and public administration. He thought he'd be there a month. But when the November hostilities broke out into an open battle for Mogadishu, Haile was trapped.

Before the artillery attack that shattered his leg, Haile sat talking with a room full of tribal elders, displaced interim government officials, lawyers, and other professionals—all Muslim. "I was the only Christian present," he said. "We were joined by a love for our people, believing that something stronger than guns could bring peace to our devastated country of Somalia."

Quite suddenly, "in an unthinkable departure from Somali morality," Aideed's military shattered Haile's quiet neighborhood. "His troops had found our meeting place!" Haile said. "Our little group of peacemakers, unarmed as we were, was a threat to Aideed's power." Occupants dashed from the house to a nearby shelter. There an anti-aircraft shell burst through the door, hitting Haile below the right knee. When his head hit the ground, he blacked out. When shells began exploding at the makeshift hospital, Haile's friends trundled him by wheelbarrow through the Bakaraha marketplace to a pickup truck. They took him to a safe house in the "Bermuda Triangle" in eastern Mogadishu.

For the next eleven days Haile became weaker. "I never stopped praying that God would let me live long enough to see my family again," Haile said. The battle for Mogadishu had knocked out international telephone service. Since the fighting had begun in November, he had been unable to contact his wife Martha in Elkhart, Indiana (U.S.). He was evacuated with the help of World Concern International. Eventually the International Red Cross flew him from

Somali boy at the Camp Liboi, a refugee camp in northern Kenya, 1993.

Mogadishu to a Nairobi hospital, where his missionary friends donated blood for his surgery and recovery. There he was finally able to telephone his family. Two days after arriving in Nairobi, Haile was considered strong enough to fly home to the States. Several Mennonite churches and agencies in Goshen covered his living and medical expenses while Haile recovered and learned to use his artificial leg.

Two years later (1994), under Eastern Mennonite Missions, Haile returned to Nairobi to teach at Daystar University College; this time his wife Martha, an African-American, and their three children joined him. "Our assignment," he wrote, "was to develop and teach a Peace Studies and Reconciliation Minor."

Haile's injuries foreshadowed other suffering and death by believers in Mogadishu.

Mennonite women in war

"Are you a Mennonite?" The tall, slim Somali refugee sitting in front of registered nurse Verda Weaver wore an eye patch. He had arrived from Ethiopia, June 1993, weary, sick, ill-clad, at a mobile medical unit in Mogadishu. "I heard that two Mennonite nurses work here," the patient said. When Verda acknowledged her heritage, he said, "When will the Mennonites open their schools?" The query was a surprise, startling but pleasant. Here, nearly 20 years after the Somalia government took over the mission schools, a refugee from out of the interior remembered the Mennonites.

Verda was one of two EMM nurses loaned to World Concern in Mogadishu, following orientation in Kenya for Somali refugee work. Marilyn Metzler was the other. Now, in January 1993, they sat in their long skirts and head scarves, not unlike the Somali women, and attended the victims of drought and warfare. The UN estimated that 100 children died every day in Mogadishu, and that three million adults in the interior needed emergency food. Verda and Marilyn provided leadership coordination and instruction to two mobile medical teams. The teams, made up primarily of Somalis, served numerous medical and nutritional needs of displaced Somali people camping in Mogadishu. But not six months into their assignment, the nurses had to be evacuated when the warlords began another fierce battle to control Mogadishu. Resting in Nairobi, Marilyn remembered a word of advice spoken by a Somali colleague: "You can't help us unless you listen to us." It was a word that liberated. "It was so freeing for me to realize that I didn't need to have all the answers," Marilyn wrote.

In June the Mennonite nurses returned to Mogadishu to pick up their work. Later, Bonnie Bergey, the EMM and MCC representative for Somalia, came from her Nairobi office for an administrative visit (February 1994). The three women stood on a flat rooftop enjoying a cool breeze from the Indian Ocean. Suddenly, an anti-tank rocket-propelled grenade shattered the calm, blasting a ten-foot hole through the two-foot thick wall. The three women threw themselves to the flat rooftop. From the street, marauders poured gunfire into the walled compound. Through the din and dust of the battle, Marilyn prayed, "God, be our shield." Later, Verda wrote, "After the attack I was keenly reminded of the risks I lived with. Yet, no place is safe outside God's will."

From Mogadishu, Marilyn later went on to Djibouti. There she nursed at a small public maternal/child hospital serving an impoverished Somali community of 150,000. Most of the patients in her 30-bed ward were malnourished children, fighting dysentery, respiratory infections, and pneumonia. Four years later (January 1998) Verda was once again in

Somalia, this time with Naomi Weaver (not a relative; Naomi spent twelve years nursing in Tanzania under EMM). As if drought and war in the North were not sufficient misery for the Somali people, unrelenting rains brought "the worst-known flooding of the lower Juba Valley." A Somali coordinator assigned Verda and Naomi to emergency health work. With Somali men poling flat-bottomed boats across the Juba River, fresh-cut channels, and flooded fields, the women helped coordinate a program of injections against a cholera epidemic.

Meanwhile, Somali newspapers in Mogadishu carried alarmingly accusatory headlines. *Wargeyska Dadka* (*The People's Newspaper*, 11/27/95) entitled an article: "The Danger that Christendom Poses to the Somali People." The anonymous article began, "Wherever the Muslim Somali people live, it is proper that they wake up and contend with the trap set for them. While relief agencies wave the flag of humanitarian aid, underneath they are spreading Christianity (infidelism)." The reporter quoted a General Caydid: "Relief organizations in the region are used to teach children the Christian religion and [immorality]." A December article stated, "Christian books written in the Somali language arrived in Mogadishu. They're called *Axdiga Cusub*, the New Testament. This is the kind broadcasted through FEBA Radio located on the Seychelles Island and is meant for misleading the Somali people."

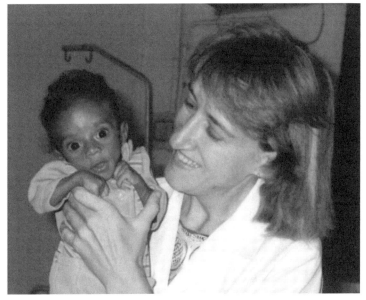

Marilyn Metzler with a child in a public maternal/child hospital in Djibouti, 1994.

Death and destruction

The 1990s: a decade in which violence ebbed and flowed. Destruction, food shortages, international aid agencies. Armed militia, armed robbers, inter-clan fighting. A quick show of power through the gun, a constant stream of displaced peoples, and clans separated or found outside their clan area. Often Somali women were left to shoulder the burdens of war; they and their children attempted to eke out a living.

Because of shifting warlord loyalties, aid workers were at high risk in the 1990s. At times they had to work outside their clan areas—outside expected protection. Further increasing their personal risk, these workers were known to have access to cash.

Many men and women died during the nineties; several in a fifteen-month period in 1994-95. These Somalis had raised questions about life. They studied Islam; they studied the *Injil* (gospel).

Early one morning, two gunmen waited on a sandy road near the Swedish Church Relief offices where Ali worked. As he approached the outside gates, the assassins shot him at close range. He was not robbed.

Months later, at a bus stop near Ahmed's home, two armed men spoke calmly to a terrified cluster of people, "Don't be frightened." But as Ahmed stepped off the bus that evening, the men gunned him down. Ahmed, who also worked at the Swedish Relief offices, had drawn encouragement from Ali. Together they stood firm in their faith, even when the risks of death became great.

Again a few months later, assassins' guns silenced another, Mohamed, found dead from gunshots. In earlier years, Mohamed had enjoyed visiting the Mennonite Mission family in Johar; he borrowed books, asked questions. Over time, Mohamed became a follower of Jesus and desired the same for his children.

And again, two gunmen broke into a Mogadishu house at night and killed Abdi and his wife in their sleep. Abdi had been an old friend of the Mennonite Mission. During his boyhood days, he met his first missionary teachers in their riverside school at Mahaddei. During those years, he became a believer. In the 1990s he left his job as an air traffic controller to work as a bookkeeper with World Concern, a non-governmental organization. When the civil war engulfed the capital, neighbors destroyed Abdi's house on the city outskirts. "I was from the wrong clan," he reported on that incident. Michael Madany of World Concern wrote (6/26/95): "Being our senior national employee during the civil war was a difficult assignment. Instead of dealing with difficult or corrupt government officials, [Abdi] now had to negotiate with drug-addicted gunmen with shifting loyalties and few scruples. Even more challenging: the warlords controlling [Abdi's] part of the city considered his clan to be enemies."

Maple leaf Somalis

Early in 1990 four Somalis found themselves as refugees in Toronto. Twenty-five years ago, they were students of the Mennonite school in Jamama. Visiting together, they recalled that their Mennonite teachers, Victor and Viola Dorsch, were Canadians. They got out the Greater Toronto telephone directory and looked up anything with Mennonite in the name. They rang the Warden Woods Mennonite Church, and the receptionist gave them the Dorsch number. Thus began the reunion of former Canadian Mennonite missionaries to Somalia and their former Somali students now living in Canada.

On July 8 of that year, several former Jamama students visited the Dorsches. A month later, at another gathering, the men urged the Dorsches to return to Jamama. "Our people need help again," they pleaded. These students connected the Dorsches to Billie Musse Shemal, the former district commissioner when they had all lived in Jamama, now also living in Canada.

Chester and Catherine Kurtz of Lancaster, Pa., started the first international gathering of Somalis and former missionaries with their October 1991 visit to their old Somali colleagues, the Dorsches, retired in Kitchener. The Kurtzes expressed interest in seeing some of their Somali friends from their Jamama and Torda days. Among the estimated 30,000 Somalis living in Toronto at that time—fleeing the civil war in their homeland—a couple dozen had close relationships with the Mennonite Mission, especially during the 1960s and 1970s.

"Cooks from a Somali restaurant served up a scrumptious meal of rice and goat meat, the food of feasts in Somalia," Chester reported. Tea, video tapes, stories. But the most poignant moment occurred when Billie Musse Shemal, representing the Somalis, and Victor Dorsch, representing the first Mennonite missionaries, asked each other for forgiveness. "Forgive us for the way some of my people often opposed your presence," Musse said. Victor said, "Forgive our poor attitudes and actions, which were too often concerned with program and property, instead of people." Two other men confessed, "When we were boys, we found wire from the mission compound fence very useful for making our toy trucks!"

Dr. Ivan and Mary Ellen Leaman made a similar visit to the Dorsches, three months later, January 1991. The generous meal of rice and goat meat, and fruits and tea, was served on tables decorated with little Somali, Canadian, and American flags. Someone was aware of the significance of the international character of this informal gathering. It, too, contributed to the formation of an association.

The Canadian Somali Friendship Association for Peace and

Development was officially formed on September 3, 1992. Billie Musse Shemal and Victor Dorsch were appointed co-chairpersons. "This friendship association is not something invented in Toronto," Musse said. "It is in our bones, a solid 40-years relationship." Other meetings of the association followed.

August 1993: Nearly a 100 people gathered, including 18 former EMM missionaries from Ohio and Pennsylvania. Dorothy Grove, widowed by an assassin in Mogadishu 30 years previous, embraced Somalis who remembered her husband Merlin and sought forgiveness. August 1995: This reunion was a time of celebration. Several families, after years of delays and bureaucracy, were allowed to join their husbands and fathers in Canada. A former student, now a lawyer, said, "We no longer have a Johar Secondary School, but we still want to live in that nostalgia."

September 1997: For the first time the reunion met at EMM headquarters in Salunga, Pa. Thirty Somalis met 50 Mennonite Mission alumni. Mohamud Togane cited Merlin and Dorothy Grove as "examples of the reconciling love so desperately needed in Somalia today." Togane said, "Merlin gave his life for Somalia—and for me."

September 2001: EMM, Salunga, again hosted the reunion of the maple leaf Somalis and their Mennonite friends.

Rhoda Salim, Ali Salim, and Mohamud Siad Togane converse at a Somali student/teacher reunion, 1997.

Decade ends with a woman

Bertha Beachy again lit a white candle that October 1997, something she had done daily since her arrival in Nairobi. "Each morning I light my white candle and pray for wisdom for myself and peace in Somalia," she said. But her October candle was more significant. Bertha lit her candle at the opening ceremonies for an extraordinary gathering, a peace workshop for women. Of the 25 Somali women meeting, eight arrived from inside Somalia; the others were refugees in Kenya.

"It was awe-inspiring for me to be part of that group," said Bertha, who addressed the gathering on three occasions. MCC contributed $5,000 to Save Somali Women and Children to hold that first-of-its-kind workshop. The diverse group of women from various clans had a common purpose: "to discuss how Somali women can foster peace instead of fueling their country's ongoing civil war."

Bertha Beachy was back in Nairobi working with Somalis after a 17-year hiatus in the States. At age 64, she took up from Bonnie Bergey the EMM and MCC administrative oversight for Somalia and Somalis elsewhere in East Africa, December 1995. Bertha learned that the Muslims' first call to prayer each morning also called her to pray as she awoke. "During grad

Bertha Beachy lights a candle in her office for peace in Somalia.

studies at Syracuse University, 1970-71, I finally understood that I was being called to pray for Somalia as I had not done before," she said. "Somali peoples call Christians to serious incarnational living in the presence of great faith."

Somali women and Somali peace were always on Bertha's Mennonite agenda in East Africa. "With various military men holding different parts of Mogadishu, the capital often is not the place to hear good news about Somalis," she wrote. "We must support Somali women working for peace." In 1997-98 MCC provided $50,000 for Somali work, most going to support women's peace conferences.

"Why women? Somali women are often married into a clan other than their own," Bertha said. "They're uniquely positioned to help resolve conflicts between clans. Most men are caught up in clan politics, but women, who frequently support their whole family financially, realize they and the children are the losers." Thus, MCC provided funds for grassroots peacemaking efforts also to women.

While EMM/MCC helped to sponsor Somalia peace conferences in Nairobi, mostly Bertha's office championed gatherings inside Somalia, in Mogadishu particularly. Among many projects, she: worked with traditional elders in peace conferences in Galcaio—the Northern part of Somalia—and the Lower Juba areas; aided schools in Mogadishu and Kismayu; assisted several Somalis to attend Eastern Mennonite University's Summer Peace Institute for training; and helped to secure positions for EMM teachers Leon and Elaine Good at Amoud University in Somaliland.

A year later, March 1999, six Somali women joined ten other women refugees from other African countries for a two-day workshop on Active Nonviolence. ANV is a system "for personal, social, national, and international change based on the forces of truth and love." Because the Somali women were Muslim, care was given to connect the ANV principles not only to Christianity, but also to Islam, Bertha reported. She, too, attended the workshop, convinced that she "needed to learn more about responding in a life-giving manner."

Like Bonnie Bergey, Bertha visited inside Somalia, always looking for ways again to connect program to the people's good memory of the earlier Mennonite Mission. November 1996, she spent a week with Willie Reimer from MCC Canada. On that visit she stood before the ruins of the Johar secondary school: roofless walls, the windows, doors, electric wires gone. The compound was a maize field guarded by women and children. Some townspeople knew of the Mennonite work 20 years ago. "We're remembered with fondness," Bertha reported. A former student said, "You people tell the truth, you don't cheat, you don't commit adultery. You are peace loving." On a four-day visit to Mogadishu with Bertha in late November 1998, Susan Godshall reinforced in her report Bertha's emphasis: "Somali women are key players in education, health, and small business developments, even among bombed buildings."

Christian peacemaker in a Muslim context

Bonnie Bergey
Former EMM and MCC Director for Somalia

Seven years ago I left my appointment as EMM and MCC's representative for Somalia, working out of Nairobi, Kenya. By now I might expect of myself a concise, analytical, descriptive study of those peacemaking efforts in Somalia. Still, I realize I have only my story, a story still trying to find words. A story of love, abuse, terror, commitment, history, and grief— all mixed together.

I believed Somalis had traditionally found ways of maintaining society and resolving conflict among themselves. So, I took on a listening role to hear from the community leaders, elders, and women. I was impressed by the culture's decision-making methods, respected elders, and designated leaders. I also began to hear how I was perceived by these people as I began to learn more of their culture and language.

First, I was perceived as "white." I could have been Canadian, American, or European. Being white carried the baggage of being a Christian in the worst sense; still remembered are the Christian Crusades which massacred thousands of Muslim peoples. Thus, being a white Christian meant that I was seen as a potential abuser of Muslim people even today. I tried to see myself as the many local Somalis might see me: an untrustworthy colleague, a bearer of violent history, an enemy of Islam.

Being "Mennonite" was the second significant perception. Over the last 50 years Mennonites have earned a reputation for integrity with the Somali people. This sometimes happened despite us or at least beyond our plans and intentions. I happened upon Somalis who either attended Mennonite secondary schools, or their brothers, sisters, or cousins were there. The names of missionary teachers are remembered with affection by young and old. The killing of a Mennonite missionary is widely recalled. I was accepted because Mennonites were known and trusted. This provided for me, a Christian, an opportunity to connect with significant local people who provided protection and housing for me wherever I went in Somalia and Somaliland—even during a war.

Being white and representing North American organizations, it was assumed that I was "wealthy." I tried to treat each request for money, projects, or other assistance with respect. I made myself listen to countless painful stories. Sometimes it was enough just to listen. Usually it took great discernment. I became known as someone who was an advocate for Somalia, but who insisted that funds be used inside Somalia itself for the good of all people.

I was seen as a "peacemaker," as the word spread that the Mennonites were back, working with various clans throughout Somalia and Somaliland, encouraging peace. The length of time I was present with them yielded trust and then bridges to peacemaking.

I was also a "threat." One warlord spoke publicly against me. Me! A Christian, a pacifist, and a woman. It seemed an honor to be known as a threat to continuing war. I felt the sense of integrity that comes with owning the choices I made. I chose to be a Christian to love and to believe wholeheartedly in a Christian presence in Somalia. Present to share both good and bad times, to walk with those who suffer. Present without needing to see an immediate outcome of peace. Present just because I am called to faithfulness by a God who is faithful.

It was painful to care. Painful to hear the story of a shopkeeper shot dead while a customer made a purchase. Painful to watch mothers selling *qat* (a widely used narcotic native to the area) because they have found no other way to feed their children. Painful to hear detailed accounts of torture in prison. Painful to hear one-by-one of the deaths of believers—to compare their cost of following Christ with my own temporary and seemingly insignificant sacrifices. I still search for healing and wholeness to know how to be faithful today, and still have strength for tomorrow.

Lancaster, Pennsylvania
October 2002

Billie Musse Shemal reminisces with Victor Dorsch at a Somali student/teacher reunion, 1994.

Toward a sustainable peace in Somalia

John Paul Lederach

Distingished Scholar and Professor of Conflict Studies,
Eastern Mennonite Univeristy
Professor of International Peacebuilding, University of Notre Dame

"If all you have is a hammer, all you see are nails." That adage described well the situation in Somalia by the end of 1992. Even with 30,000 international troops in the country, we could not rely exclusively on the hammers of food relief and its secure delivery. We needed tools that helped to bring sustainable reconciliation for Somalis. We needed a comprehensive, creative approach to restoring peace that addressed both immediate humanitarian concerns and the long-term challenges of transforming conflict.

Now, a decade later, I feel even more strongly that the additional tools acquired then for our toolbox continue to be the following:

1. Whenever food is needed immediately, and mechanisms for its delivery negotiated with respective parties, the urgency should not be used as leverage to push for an immediate, high-profile, internationally convened peace conference of select Somalis.

Somalia does not need a trickle-down approach to peace. Somali reconciliation must instead be based on regional subclan and interclan consultations that build toward a national forum. Over the past decade, such efforts have occurred in numerous regions. They were well-documented and attended by international observers. All working for Somalia's betterment should continue to encourage and support the logistics involved in local and regional peace conferences, eventually building toward a national conference.

2. Negotiating with those who control guns was crucial so food could be delivered immediately. But it was not the key to long-term peace. Focus on armed groups only enhances their status and power. Long-term transformation must continue to create a Somali peace constituency that serves as an infrastructure for reconciliation. In Somali society that infrastructure lies with the traditional elders, intellectuals for peace, religious leaders, poets, traders, and women. Key cultural and historical institutions unique to Somalis must continue to be given more power and integrated into the peace process.

3. Somalia is an oral society. The international community should continue to work at building a "radio-for-peace" that provides regular and unbiased information about the peace process. More needs to be accomplished for sustainable peace with regular, objective information via radio—airing regional peace conference reports, poetry for peace, advocacy for dialogue from elders and religious leaders, and concrete details of humanitarian relief and reconstruction projects.

4. Relief and reconstruction efforts must be linked with serious programs for disarmament. That challenge, where successfully met, shows the possibility of shifting from sustenance by gun to sustenance by work, and eventually a civil government. A comprehensive approach to peace must create alternatives to militarization. This cannot be limited to a mere formula of food for weapons. A broader socioeconomic view of the situation includes development and employment in exchange for weapons. Particularly gratifying are those programs that successfully target youth.

5. Likewise, the cycle of weapons and munitions entering Somalia must be addressed with equal seriousness. Humanitarian concern for fractured Somali life is cynical and naive if it is not accompanied with clear efforts for stopping those who simultaneously fuel the conflict behind the clan violence and profit from it through weapons sales and trafficking.

Nederland, Colorado
October 2002

My Somali sojourn

Bertha Beachy
Former EMM and MCC Representative for Somalia

September 2002: I met Somalis everywhere as soon as I landed in the Twin Cities (Minneapolis and Saint Paul, Minn.). They were walking in the streets, driving taxis, selling in the malls, eating in restaurants and coffee shops. It amazed me to see some of the estimated 50,000 Somalis living in one of the coldest spots in America. Somali conversation had not changed—I loved it!

September 1958: I swung off the Africa oceanliner onto a small tender in Mogadishu's open harbor. Thus began my odyssey with these dignified, loquacious, and often complex Somalis. With my degree barely dry, I began an English day school and later a bookstore. I will never be the same—I pray and fast differently because of their Islamic fervor.

I learned a great deal of grammar with my adult students. After nationalization, I taught in three secondary schools. One had Russian KGB agents among the teachers. In 1974 the Somali government sent me to Lafoole, the College of Education begun by an American University. I was the one American Christian woman among some 60 teachers on campus. I loved it! Eventually, all the Mennonite teachers were sent out of Somalia. I felt bereft of everything. I moved to Kenya and

managed the production of three Somali language primers for the National Christian Council of Kenya. I left Africa in July 1978.

December 1995: I returned to Kenya to administer the Somali desk for both EMM and MCC. Each day, believers, refugees, and old friends trooped through my office. Fighting among the warlords continued in southern Somalia. Every visit inside the country required the protection of a Somali non-government organization and a full complement of AK-47s both behind and in front of my vehicle. Only once did I briefly walk outside without guns. I wept for the people and for Mogadishu.

I learned that tending my own spirit helped me know the nudges of the Holy Spirit in each request. Sometimes my compassion trapped me. How could I continue to relate to persons who deceived me? I carefully scattered my bit of aid among different clans and areas. Much of the aid helped build a future. My hope grew as I spent a day in Djibouti at the formation of The Transitional National Government, which returned to Mogadishu, October 2000.

Each Saturday believers met for Bible study in Nairobi. Clan problems affected many of these refugees, as did the differing theological beliefs of missionaries. Amazing faith resided next to overwhelming survival needs. A gathering in

Ethiopia brought believers together from different parts of the world. I insisted that at least one woman lead a devotional, to demonstrate that the Holy Spirit builds the body of Christ not only with men.

Mostly, my hope for peace lies with the Somali women. Middle-aged Marian reminded me that her training began in 1960 in the day school and hospital in Jamama. Today she has eleven living children, she manages six small clinics for a foreign NGO (non-government organization), and she delivers babies in her home for women who cannot get across the green line of safety in Mogadishu to the hospital. Asha works in cross-clan peacemaking with Somali women. She invited me to her home for a Muslim anointing with oil for an injured friend. Fatima works in a rural area with the environment. She integrates her training in peace issue skills for both young men and women. Raha manages schools for children through eighth grade.

Daily I hold my Somali prayer beads and pray for peace among Somalis. Somalis alone can change their future. But the Unites States and five other countries must stop selling guns to Somalis. This counters a 1995 resolution. May God be merciful to all of us.

Goshen, Indiana
September 2002

Two thousand & beyond

Call to prayer

"Pray that God will work through this current peace initiative to restore a lasting peace in Somalia.

"Pray that the civil society will put aside clan differences and include all the players in the conference.

"Pray especially for Somali women, who care deeply about a future for their children."

In April 2000, Bertha Beachy thought that EMM should issue a special call for prayer to its constituent churches. Why this sense of urgency?

A broad new initiative for Somali peace was taking place in the Horn of Africa during March through early May 2000. The previous year, Somali women wrote a letter to Kofi Annan, secretary general of the UN, urging him to renew UN efforts to work again for peace in Somalia. Later, the Organization for African Unity asked its Intergovernmental Authority on Development to assign Ismail Omar Guelleh to work with Somalia. Guelleh, the president of Djibouti, is an ethnic Somali. By March 2000, he convened more than 60 Somali civic leaders. In April, the traditional and religious elders from major clans arrived at Arta, 20 miles from Djibouti. Anticipating May, when participants at the peace conference would be more than 1000 with at least 100 women included, when the negotiators would begin the intense work of writing

an interim three-year constitution, Bertha discussed with EMM officials the vision of a call to prayer. Joining Bertha, Susan Godshall, Jewel Showalter, and Barbara Witmer compiled "Calling the Church to Prayer for Somalia: May 7, 2000."

The document suggested practical ways to stand with Somalis beyond the special day, May 7: offer corporate congregational prayers for Somalia each Sunday in May; enjoin small groups, cell groups, mid-week prayer meetings to remember the suffering people of Somalia, daily and weekly during May; fast for the noon meal on Sunday, May 7; indeed, set aside every Friday noontime (the Muslim holy day) for special fasting and prayers for Somalia. Most Lancaster Conference churches and many churches in neighboring conferences heeded the call for prayer. Bertha reported from Nairobi, "When I told a Somali friend that Lancaster Conference churches were being called to special prayer for his country during May, he nearly cried with gratitude."

Accompanying the Call to Prayer, a suggested pastoral prayer for public or private use, employed these lines:

God of Abraham and Sarah, Isaac and Rebecca,
God of Merlin Grove, David Miller, Peter John Leaman,
Evelyn Wesselhoeft, and God of our Somali friends,
We come before you today on behalf of the people of Somalia,
You have seen their suffering for more than nine years of

Anarchy and clan warfare.
They have suffered because of colonial powers, the Cold War,
And their own leaders, as well as famine, droughts, and floods.
Have mercy, we pray, and hearken to the blood of innocents
That cry out to you from the earth...
Where there has been violence and revenge
Bring the power to heal and the grace to forgive;
Where there has been hurt and hardness
Soften hearts to hope and hear;
Where there has been grief and greed
Plant joy and generosity
Where there has been selfishness and hate
Rain down love and hospitality....

Abdourahman, assistant principal at the Lycée d'Etat de Djibouti (high school), with Michael and Cindy Brislen.

In August, the newly selected president and 90 parliamentarians arrived in Mogadishu to a tumultuous crowd of greeters. There began, then, the hard task of convincing doubters that this was not one more warlord come to the capital.

Next door to the Djibouti peace conference, Leon and Elaine Good taught at the newly established Amoud University in Somaliland—Leon, science; Elaine, English. Between them they taught the entire student body of more than 100 students, and six of the 17 courses offered that semester. "Your presence has been a tremendous morale boost for the university," declared its president, Professor Suleiman Ahmed Guled.

People of God

A Somali youth came at night—not unlike Nicodemus—to David Shenk, his school principal at Johar, with a cautious query about Jesus. "I am a Muslim but I am reading your Bible. It is hard. Do you have a study guide?" That query in 1966 sent David on a search to find a simple Bible study appropriate for Muslims on a personal journey. Finding nothing suitable, David began to write one in his spare time. "I did not work alone," he noted. "A small team met with me over a school break. We did this together. The draft was mimeographed and well-received."

In 1973 when some missionaries were dismissed from Somalia, David convened a committee of eight in Nairobi to revise the course. "All were believers in the Messiah," David wrote. "Two had advanced degrees in Islamic studies. We met weekly. We tested each chapter with Muslims for feedback and critique. We also asked the head of the Ahamadiyya Muslim Mission in Nairobi for his assessment. The process of writing, testing, and revising took four years."

The resulting four booklets—The Beginning of People, God's Covenant with People, God Loves People, and The People of Faith—take readers through the Bible from Genesis to Revelation. "The genius of the course," David noted, "is that it is based primarily on those scriptures which the Qur'an honors as revealed scripture: The Torah, the Psalms, and the Gospel. In light of the Qur'anic injunction that Christians should make their scriptures available without price, the *People of God* (POG) team recommends that whenever a person requests this course, that the person also receives a free copy of the scripture upon which the course is based."

Director Bishop Joash Osiro, a 10-year veteran of working with POG, holds a graduate degree in Islamics from a British university. Together with his wife Rebecca, they have their hands full corresponding with a thousand students a year in East Africa. In addition, they work with churches in East Africa to follow up with the correspondence students, give seminars on Islam to church leaders, and work on new POG initiatives, according to Darren and Cindi Schaupp, EMM assistants in the office.

Mark Logan talks with women in Juba Valley, 2002.

Translated into 40 languages, from A to Y—Afar to Yoruba—the POG books continue to be in high demand. Darren noted, "Understandably, since the study was written with a Muslim religious worldview, the culturally sensitive, invitational approach has made POG acceptable and interesting among Muslim peoples around the world."

On one of Rebecca's field trips to meet with students and ministry leaders, the idea for POG's latest project was sprung. "Women expressed significant interest in learning more about the Bible," she reported. Unfortunately, in East Africa many women are not literate and have no way to study such materials on their own. So, the vision to put the POG materials in audio format was born. In May 2001, Joash traveled to the Mennonite Media Studios in Harrisonburg, Va., to record POG in Swahili.

Elsewhere on the Somalia Mennonite scene for 2001:

On Labor Day, EMM headquarters, Salunga, Pa., again hosted the "Friends of Somalia Mennonite Mission." Around 20 Somalis from Toronto, Kitchener, Milwaukee, Chicago, and Baltimore met nearly 40 retired and former EMM workers in Somalia living in the Lancaster area.

Chantal and Mark Logan began a second year as representatives in Nairobi for EMM and MCC Somali interests. Previously they worked in Djibouti, Mark doing computer maintenance for the Ministry of Education and serving as mission director, Chantal teaching French. On a brief visit to

Bishop Joash Osiro works with Justin Mitchell, an engineer at Mennonite Media, to record the People of God Bible lessons.

Mogadishu, Chantal reported that the city looked like Europe after World II. "When Somalia becomes stable again, will there be a Marshall Plan for Somalia, in which the Mennonites might be involved in helping to rebuild the country?"

The EMM Somalia office in Nairobi continued to relate to and encourage various groups of Somalis in Mogadishu and in Nairobi.

AIDS and SAACID

"The closing ceremony for the January (2002) AIDS workshop in Mogadishu was joyful, one filled with speeches, poems, songs, and dances," wrote Chantal Logan (co-representative of EMM and MCC with her husband Mark), reporting on the conference from Nairobi. Somali women's organizations planned and led the workshop. Single, married, and widowed women, ages 17 to 55, arrived from urban and rural areas, the attendance growing from 30 to 80 over the four days.

The MCC-funded workshop helped to break the silence surrounding AIDS. A decade of war, which shattered public healthcare services and broke traditional family morality, resulted in the rise of AIDS in Somalia. Few wanted to admit the problem in this predominately Muslim country. To do so suggested that their people no longer lived by Islam's strict moral code.

"A nurse gave an overview of HIV and AIDS and explained how they are spread," Chantal reported. Women were encouraged to share experiences, stories, and the rumors surrounding AIDS. Chantal was impressed with how the Somali workshop facilitators handled such material "wisely and with great sensitivity."

A large banner decorating the hall where the meeting took place bore the names MCC and EMM. The name "Mennonite Mission" received the highest mark of tribute that Somalis bestow: a praise-poem by a female poet attending the workshop.

> I wish for Mennonite Mission a life of peace,
> To have a thankful and better life.
> I pray to God for Mennonite Mission's success—
> Never to meet enemies.
> If there comes an enemy, may God intervene.
> Mennonite Mission in Somali society,
> You have a famous name.
> When Somalis hear your name, they are very grateful.
> The crops you planted in Somalia long, long ago—
> Many are bearing their fruits now.

"In a time when Christians and Muslims seem to be in contention, it is worthy to note that Mennonites were greatly honored in this devoutly Muslim country," Logan observed.

A generation of Somali children has never known peace. Few have attended school. They play war games that imitate the life they grew up in. But SAACID (the acronym means "helping" in the Somali language) leaders refused to neglect Somali children. Founded in 1996 with 37 children in Mogadishu, in an abandoned Italian colonial-era building, SAACID grew to school 343 students in grades 1 to 10 by 2002.

"Building on decades of Mennonite-Somali cooperation

SAACID school in Mogadishu.

in education," Rachel Beth Miller, an MCC writer, stated, "MCC's Global Family Program provides scholarships for 50 SAACID students. At least half are girls, all are orphans, and all have the potential to build a peaceful Somalia." Several of the SAACID teachers were educated in schools run by EMM during the 1950s—1970s. "Some use a peacemaking curriculum they designed and are enthusiastic about teaching conflict resolution skills."

"Seeds and fish hooks help proclaim peace, too," declared Mark Logan. Inter-clan violence burned 13 villages—1,200 families lost everything, "including hooks, lines, and nets they needed to fish in the Juba River." MCC sponsored conflict mediation and bought $6,000 worth of fishing equipment. Each family received two hooks and 300 feet of line. "Although the area is still poor, malnutrition slowly decreased," Logan noted. Elsewhere, seeds and simple tools were distributed just in time for the new planting season.

"Yes, our Mennonite aid has saved people's lives and allowed them to remain in their homelands," Logan wrote. "But even more importantly, we need to help more people to be trained as peacemakers. Only seeds planted in love and watered by the grace of God will bring forth a harvest. This knowledge keeps Mennonites working in a country that has demoralized many. It is faith that keeps us going when the world around us seems to have gone suddenly mad."

Mennonite advocacy for Somalia

Fatima Jibrell
Managing Director
Horn Relief Organization

As a Somali woman from pastoral background and environment and an environmental activist, I am happy to have established a reliable relationship with the Mennonites. Mennonites are a group with a vision of Muslim and non-Muslim understanding, cooperation, linking and learning from each other.

The main activities of Mennonites in Somalia before 1970 was education. One notices now the many middle-aged men who owe their schooling to Mennonite schools, in particular the Shebelli Secondary School of Johar.

During the last twelve years of civil crisis, Mennonites have remained active in supporting Somali civil society organizations, refugee families in Kenya, and most of all, they have advocated for Somali issues. They also promote understanding among Muslims in the United States.

Mennonite volunteers and workers visit civil society organizations inside Somalia, risking their lives for solidarity and visualizing the real happenings on the ground.

Mennonites do not support all organizations in monetary terms, but they are kind and concerned in listening, advocating, and most of all, understanding the Somali peoples' struggles, pain, and dreams.

Mennonites are culturally sensitive and humble. They eat with us from the same plate and sleep with us on the same floor. We wish other humanitarian partner institutions could learn from them.

This will remain with me forever: my travel to New York for United Nations meetings and to Washington, D.C., moving from one meeting to another, doing public relations speaking in support of Somalia, hoping to influence major decisions.

During all these activities, people from the Mennonite advocacy offices in Washington and the New York Mennonite guest house have been my major facilitators and organizers. Bertha Beachy is one of those who cultivated this long process of love and support to Somalis by the Mennonites. May Allah keep this relationship productive.

Buran, Northern Somalia
September 2002

The work goes on

Donald R. Jacobs
Missionary Statesman

Having sent missionaries to "animist" Tanzania and "Orthodox" Ethiopia following World War II, the Mennonites thought, "Why not Muslim Somalia?"

East Africa and the Horn presented a new frontier for the Mennonites. They had never placed missionaries in Islamic lands so had little idea of what lay ahead of them. Somalia presented unusual challenges to their flexibility. It would prove to cost them heavily in life and resources.

Their plan was simple—serve the Somali people through education, medicine, and development. That was the tried and proven method employed by missions all over the world at the time. They did not intend to plant churches in Somalia. That made this venture unique. Somalia was totally Muslim.

The Mennonite Mission efforts to serve the nation succeeded. In due course they planted institutions—the modern Jamama Hospital, the attractive educational programs for adults in Mogadishu and the stellar Shebelli Secondary School in Johar. These modern services won the praise of many. Clearly, the Mennonite Mission touched a felt need in Somali culture. However, their "success" drew too much attention to themselves. The high visibility made them uncomfortable because they had determined to work unobtrusively. As expected, their efforts alarmed Muslim purists. The struggle was engaged.

The missionaries played down the Christian aspect of their work. For example, Qur'anic teachers provided religious education in their schools as the law required. The missionaries were there to serve and that was that. They determined to do what was necessary to maintain a presence in that rapidly developing nation. The Islamic religious hierarchy was similarly determined to neutralize the effects of the mission.

As time went on, a few individuals began to ask the missionaries to explain their understanding of Jesus. The missionaries were, understandably, very discreet about verbalizing their faith. Inevitably, however, some Somali individuals believed.

That stirred the waters. But the tidal wave struck when a few Somalis baptized one another in the Indian Ocean without the knowledge of the missionaries. Religious leaders took notice. Private beliefs could be tolerated, to some degree, but water baptism was unacceptable.

For a while the religious leaders endured the Mennonite Mission because of the benefits the mission brought to the nation. Over time, political and religious dynamics led to the expulsion of missionaries in 1976. In 1980 Mennonites were again invited into Somalia so the Mennonite Central Committee provided personnel to help refugees and in 1981 EMM again sent teachers.

This story is the drama of the interplay between two distinct worldviews, that of the Islamic host culture, and the culture of the missionaries, which was seen as representing Western Christianity. The story reveals the challenge that the Mennonite Mission presented to Somali culture and religion and the cost of restraint, commitment, and personal sacrifice on the part of missionaries and believers.

The story goes on. The future chapters will no doubt also feature the Somalis in diaspora, as God continues his good work among them, and among all Somali peoples.

Landisville, Pennsylvania
November 2002

Mark and Chantal Logan meet with faculty at Amoud University, Boroma, Somaliland, 2001.

Afterword: What's in a name?

Of clans and ancestors: lessons to be learned from the Somali-Mennonite story

Chantal and Mark Logan
EMM and MCC representatives to Somali People

The Somali people traditionally memorize the name of their fathers, grandfathers, great-grandfathers up to the twentieth generation. One of the purposes of that memorization was, and is today, identification. When one Somali met another in the bush, the exchange of names was proof of family lineage and assured safe passage. But with the names that were memorized there also came a story, usually the tale of the founding ancestor who had given his name to the clan.

In many of those stories, such as those about the founder of the Darood clan, the ancestor had fled the prestigious land on the Arabian Peninsula, the homeland of the Prophet Mohamed. In some of the legends, the founding ancestor had fled to the African continent to escape the reach of a pursuer. After he suffered from thirst and hunger, God miraculously fed the fugitive who then, taking a bride from the new land, founded a Somali clan.

In other stories, such as those about the Yibir clan, the founding ancestor came as a missionary of Islam, bringing the light of monotheism to a polytheist people. As in the story of Elijah and the prophets of Baal, the ancestor had challenged the power of the traditional belief and had come away the victor, establishing the superiority of the new religion. Whether any historical truth hides behind these stories is a matter of debate for anthropologists, but for us, factual history is not the point. These stories reveal truth that both Mennonite Christians and Somali Muslims can readily embrace.

Somalis and Mennonites will agree on the importance of identifying themselves in the broader context of community rather than as isolated human beings. For those of us who live in strongly individualistic societies, the stories of our past remind us that our generation has not created itself and that the world around us existed well before we entered it. Our individual names and lives only have meaning in the light of the long list of those who have preceded us. As Christians, we know from Hebrews 11 that we are the descendants in faith of a great cloud of witnesses, who, though departed, cheer us on as we continue in the journey of our shared belief. What we reap today is the fruit of seed others have sown.

In our work as Mennonite representatives to the Somali people, we are constantly reminded of this truth. Whether or not Somalis respect us as Chantal and Mark Logan, we never cease to be awed by how they regard the name "Mennonite."

Their faces light up with recognition. Suddenly we are not just some westerners, working for one more international non-government organization. We are people they know because "our ancestors" are not strangers to them. The name of our lineage, the Mennonite Mission clan, is the seal of our acceptance and a form of safe passage without our needing first to prove ourselves as individuals.

But the stories of the past also tell us of God's special provision when sending his people to a strange land. For the Mennonites, it may not have been food or water that God miraculously provided when they arrived in Somalia, but we are convinced that it was divine intervention that brought Mennonites and Somalis together, and allowed them to live together with respect and mutual appreciation as religious people from very different theological backgrounds. It was God in his wisdom who brought Christians from a history and background of community into the midst of this Islamic society. And it was God in his faithfulness who gave the Mennonites courage and the will to maintain a viable presence even as trouble and hardship emerged. And it was God the Gardener who tended Mennonite life and death in Somalia, and from that seed brought forth the fruit of the ancestral name of Mennonite in Somalia.

It might be good to reflect a bit on why God chose to

Chantal Logan with students at Mercy School, 2002.

send conservative, Lancaster County Mennonites to the Somali people in 1953. There may be some lesson we can learn, to guide us further along the way. We can only speculate on the mind of God, but using the rational minds he has given us, we see missiological wisdom in this plan. It is perhaps ironic, that what is sometimes amusing to the newcomers and sometimes interpreted as Mennonite exclusiveness could be seen as a positive point of commonality for Mennonites in the land of the Somali. The Mennonite understanding of identity is somewhat akin to that of the Somalis, as illustrated in the famous "Mennonite name game." The way Mennonites who meet for the first time start reciting family names in search of a close family relationship is not unlike what Somalis do when they meet at the well or at the crossing of trails in the bush.

Adding to a communal sense of identity, and playing the family name game, a conservative way of life was also a point of unity. With the abstinence of drinking alcohol and a modest dress for the women, the early Mennonites stood in sharp contrast to other "infidels" from the West being observed by the Somali people. The expatriate community in Somalia, as in most parts of Africa, has never been known for its high moral standards. Among the Italian colonizers in Somalia, only priests and nuns made any effort to observe the strict moral standards required of Muslims or to live a life of service. Mennonites, however, who while striving for a radical discipleship to their Prophet Jesus, were allowed to marry and have families, if they so chose, were seen as a religious people to whom the Somalis could relate. This lifestyle approval helped Mennonites overcome the obstacle of skin color, which at first sight identified them as *gaal* or infidel.

Even more, it was their allegiance to one particular teaching of their Messiah which made Mennonites well-suited

for the call of God laid upon their lives. A theology of peace and nonviolence placed Mennonites in a position "to give the reason for the hope within them" (1 Pet. 3:15) in a gentle and respectful way. The Anabaptist belief that peace is the very heart of the gospel prepared Mennonites to witness in non-aggressive ways to a Muslim people, a people for whom the Christian message has always been tainted by the blood of the Crusades. That same belief gives us credibility even today, in the aftermath of the September 11 and October 7* attacks, which have brought the Crusades mentality flying back at us with vengeance.

And loyalty to the Anabaptist heritage gave Mennonites the will and courage to stand firm under hardship and testing in the Horn of Africa. A knowledge and understanding of the history and beliefs of their "founding ancestors" informed the Mennonite clan on how to react when challenges came from governing authorities. Faced with first, a government restriction on preaching their faith, then with a government mandate to permit Islam to be taught in their schools, Mennonites found in their past a model for remaining present in society, and true to their faith, despite adverse government requirements.

In the world, but not of the world. The Anabaptist experience and understanding of being a witnessing community, in submission to, but not in agreement with, ruling authorities, presented Mennonite missionaries with a viable alternative to leaving Somalia, when others decided they could not stay. We have been told by Somali friends that it was then that true colors were shown. Mennonites indeed had come to educate and to serve. Their main concern was to be a faithful witness, not to proselytize, and therefore could be trusted. Again we see how God provides for the people he sends, this time with events centuries ahead of the time they were called to be in, the right people in the right place.

Yet, surely, if the whole story were to be told, one would discover that the Mennonites who served in Somalia were no less sinners than others. They were not devoid of prejudices and misconceptions about African people, and if they were indeed a community, there was plenty of grumbling and bickering in their midst. But as the story is told and the book is written, it becomes clear that it was God's grace which prepared them, it was God's grace which carried them through, and it is God's grace which has today given Mennonites the harvest of a known and respected name in the land where they lived as missionaries of Light.

It is, however, unfortunate that the harvest of a respected name is not what captures the attention of people in the Western world these days. Even Mennonites can be influenced by the prevailing values of the culture around them, and many tend to see numbers as being all important. Yet, for it to be an honor in an Islamic state to be introduced as a representative of the Mennonite Mission, and for the Mennonite Mission to be blessed in the poetry of a society that sees itself as 100 percent Muslim is a gift which cannot be taken lightly, and especially when it is so clearly a gift from God. God may have given us this gift in reward for the obedience and faithfulness of our predecessors, but we believe, in all humility, the real gift is to the Somali people, and it is a gift that has not yet been fully received.

As many who have not had Muslims as neighbors are just now discovering Islam, it might be significant to point out that there is a category worse than the infidel in Islam: the hypocrite, someone who pretends to be something he is not. A hypocrite calls himself by a false name or disguises his true identity. Mennonites in Somalia have never hidden their identity. We don't make a point to introduce ourselves as Christians, since Christianity has many connotations today which do not represent the teachings of Jesus, and using these terms can be offensive to Muslims. Yet, Somalis know we are followers of Jesus. They sometimes say, "Yes, we know Mennonites are Christians, but they are the good kind." We have always been thankful that Mennonites have had the wisdom and fortitude to

Mark and Chantal Logan (left) and Bertha Beachy (right) with Somali friends in Nairobi, 2000.

be open and transparent about who they are, and even under the pressure to produce numbers, have not sold their birthright for a plate of beans.

What about the future? Any Somali, or any African, will tell you that the worst thing that can happen to a name is for it to disappear. And your name is only forgotten when you cease to have descendants who carry your name. Being forgotten by your descendants is worse than death, for time is more than a few short life spans. Polygamy is allowed, as fathering many children will keep your name alive for many generations. So, as we stand at the threshold of this jubilee year, 2003, we look around us and we wonder: where are our descendants who will carry the torch for the next 50 years? At this moment we don't see a long line of people waiting to give their lives to God in Somalia, but we believe that God, as before, is preparing workers for his harvest. Is it that we can't see them because they have not been challenged to come forward, or could it be that we are looking at the wrong places?

Still one last thing remains for us to learn from the stories of clans and founding ancestors. According to some Somali experts (Gunther Schlee and Abdi Mohamed Mohamed), the very notion of clan is not only a biological affiliation. A weaker clan can join a stronger one and then adopt its name. It is called *sheegad*, which means that one accepts to tell the names of the ancestors of the stronger clan when asked to give the names of his own forefathers.

One thing this practice shows us is that to be part of the Mennonite clan one does not necessarily need to be white, North American, or to come from Lancaster County. It is not a question of ethnicity; it is a question of claiming a name. But something more in *sheegad* strikes a deep chord in our understanding of the Christian faith. For what is the name of our founding ancestor, the name which gives us Life? What is the name that makes us part of the clan of the redeemed? No, it is not the name Victor Dorsch, neither the name Menno Simons, but it is the name Jesus Christ.

It is our hope and our prayer that the name Mennonite Mission will live long in Somalia, not for the sake of Mennonites but for the Somali people. It is our yearning that they will have an enduring sign post pointing to that other name, the Name above all names, the ancient name of the One whose return we await together. A road marker leading to that only name by which we can ever be saved from the chaos and conflict of this world and that name which will open, to Mennonites and Somalis alike, the way into the world to come.

Nairobi, Kenya
October 2002

* On September 11, 2001, commercial airliners were hijacked and deliberately crashed into three large office buildings in two American cities. On October 7, the United States and Great Britain attacked 30 targets across Afghanistan. As the U.S. is generally considered to be a Christian nation and Afghanistan is an Islamic state, many voices from around the world have identified these related attacks as a renewal of an old religious conflict between Christianity and Islam. —the Logans

Appendices

A 50-year time line

1950

January:
Orie O. Miller, executive secretary of Eastern Mennonite Board of Missions and Charities (EMBMC), suggests a visit to Somalia.

October:
Mahlon Hess and Dr. Merle Eshleman, senior EMBMC Tanganyika missionaries, visit Somalia and recommend steps to establish a Mission there.

1951

March:
EMBMC accepts Hess and Eshleman's recommendation at Annual Meeting.

1952

February:
Miller joins Eshleman on a second exploratory visit to Somalia.

1953

January:
Wilbert and Rhoda Lind, with son Daniel, arrive in Mogadiscio.

March:
First Sunday worship service organized by the Mission.
Fae Miller, R.N., and Caroline Plank arrive to study Somali.

June:
Wilbert Lind visits South Jubaland to explore sites of former Swedish Lutheran missionary activities.

November:
Lind begins first evening English/Bible class with 12 men.

1954

June:
Lind and Miller visit Mahaddei Uen; decide to establish first inland station there: an elementary school for boys, and a clinic.

1955

December:
Ground-breaking ceremony for school on leased land at Mahaddei Uen. Roy and Edna Shirk begin construction.

1956

January:
Agricultural demonstrations begin at Torda village.

March:
The Carl Wesselhoeft family takes up residence in Mahaddei.

1957

February:
Helen Landis, R.N., opens clinic in Mahaddei.

July:
Missionary families rent duplex in Jamama during construction of homes, clinic, and school on site north of town. Victor and Viola Dorsch begin English classes in the town and make visits to riverine villages of former Swedish believers.

1958

January:
Evelyn Wesselhoeft, five-week-old child of Carl and Leota Wesselhoeft, dies due to illness.

1959

March:
Mogadiscio missionaries move into newly-purchased property beside the fairgrounds on Afgoi Road.

July:
Five-member deputation team arrives from Tanganyika Mennonite Church to evaluate needs in Lower Juba among Swahili-speaking villages.

August:
Fellowship is renewed with former Swedish Lutheran believers. Day school opens in Jamama.

October:
Rhoda Lind attacked by night-time assailant.

1960

March:
Six-month old Peter John Leaman, son of Ivan and Mary Ellen, dies due to illness.

June/July:
British Somaliland and Italian Somalia granted independence, joining together on July 1 to form an independent Somali Republic.

August:
PAX agriculture program at Torda discontinued.

1961

March:
Twenty-five bed hospital opens at Jamama.

October:
Resettlement scheme for Bartire clan begins at Noleye.

1962

March:
Somali government suspends all of the Mission's activities.

April:

Construction of Johar Intermediate School begins.

July:

Somali government revokes suspension of activities. Clinics and hospital open first; later, the schools.

July:

Merlin Grove dies Friday, July 16, from stab wounds by assailant; Mogadishu burial. His wife Dorothy is stabbed also, but recovers.

December:

EMBMC President Raymond Charles attends luncheon at White House, invited by President Kennedy, on the occasion of Somalia's prime minister's visit to Washington.

1963

June:

Somalia's national assembly ratifies change to Article 29 (Freedom of Religion) of the constitution to ban "propagandizing of religions other than Islam."

July:

Johar Intermediate Boarding School opens.

September:

Somali government decides that all schools must permit the teaching of Islam. Joint meeting of the EMBMC Board and the Lancaster Bishop Board grants permission. Sudan Interior Mission (SIM) closes schools. The Chester Kurtz family collides with giraffe in Kenya; wife Catherine hospitalized with brain concussion.

November:

Somali government refuses $200 million offer from West for military assistance; accepts $300 million from Russia.

1964

January:

EMBMC considers expansion into Hargeisa (capital of former British Somaliland) and Djibouti, French Somaliland.

February:

New Africa Bookshop opens at Mogadishu.

March:

Border incidents with Ethiopia erupt into open war in Ogaden.

April:

Somalia's national elections: 21 political parties form.

June:

David Miller, builder, dies in motorcycle crash.

October:

Somalia minister of State informs the Mission that it must cease teaching Somali citizens the Christian faith.

1965

May:

Mennonite Mission team joins government emergency medical efforts in ministering to famine victims in Galcaio.

1966

June:

The Somali fellowships choose elders.

July:

New Africa Bookshop moves to rented quarters on Parliament Square, changes name to New Africa Booksellers.

October:

Sudan Interior Mission (SIM) missionaries in Mogadishu complete translation of the New Testament into Somali.

1968

May:

The Jamama Hospital Nurse-Dresser School inaugurates two-year program.

August:

Mission opens in rented facilities in Kismayu.

September:

Mennonite Economic Development Association (MEDA) contributes to rural development projects, particularly in the Mahaddei area.

December:

Ten-day Bible study held at Johar.

1969

February:

The German Evangelical Churches donate two million shillings to build a secondary school at Johar.

October

Somali President Shermarke assassinated. Revolutionary Council seizes power, disbanding parliament. Major-General Mohamed Siad Barre emerges as leader.

1970

January:

Mahaddei community development program launched.

January:

Government changes name to Somali Democratic Republic.

July:

United States Agency for International Development (USAID) ends aid to Somalia.

1971

February:
Shebelli Secondary School, Johar, opens with 200 students.

1972

October:
The government nationalizes the Mission's schools and medical facilities. Government also announces the use of Latin script for writing the Somali language.

December:
The government requests that all missionary medical personnel and teachers with religion degrees leave the country. Properties, facilities, and equipment nationalized without compensation. Remaining missionary teachers vacate mission housing for rented facilities. John and Velma Zook leave Mahaddei/Johar after construction projects are nationalized.

1973

March:
Several former missionaries to Somalia now work in Islamic ministries based in Nairobi, Kenya.

July:
Robert and Betty Lou Buckwalter, community development workers, are asked to leave Mahaddei.

1974

August:
Nationwide literacy campaign mounted by government.

September:
Sudan Interior Mission withdraws from Somalia.

November:
The government orders mission administrators who are not teachers also to leave the country.

1975

July:
Commissioning of first Somali leader/shepherd, Mogadishu.

1976

April:
Somali Minister of Education informs Mennonite teachers that their services are no longer needed. Last missionary teachers leave May 20.

July:
Several former missionaries to Somalia now relocated to work with Somalis in Kenya's Northeastern Province.

1977

January:
Somali troops join with Somalis living in Ethiopia to 'liberate' the Ogaden; skirmishes escalate into full-scale war.

With translation of Old Testament completed by SIM missionaries in Ethiopia, the entire Bible is now available in the Somali language.

November:
Russians expelled from Somalia.

1980

Border war with Ethiopia displaces 1.3 million Somalis; 750,000 in refugee camps. Mennonite Central Committee (MCC) sends its first aid workers.

1981

February
Somali government requests that Mennonite teachers return to Somalia.

December
First EMM teachers return to Mogadishu on government assignments.

1983

August
Other former teachers also return to Mogadishu.

1985

Dorothy Grove visits Mogadishu after twenty-three years.

1986

Beginning of three-year influx of Mennonites into agriculture, nutrition, and other community development projects: Mogadishu, Merka, Kismayu.

1987

MCC opens work with refugees in South Juba.

1988

War with Ethiopia collapses.

1989

EMM missionaries study French for assignment in Djibouti.

September
MCC withdraws all workers from Somalia because of rising interclan and subclan violence. MCC International Conciliation Service joins *Ergada Wadatashiga Somaliyeed* (Somali Peace

and Consultation Committee) for cross-clan dialogue.

1990
January
    EMM places nine teachers in Mogadishu area.
December
    All EMM missionaries leave Somalia for Nairobi, Kenya, due to mounting civil war.

1991
Spring
    Clan-based militias drive Gen. Siad Barre from power. Factions vie for control of the South. Somaliland secedes.

1992
September
    Canadian Somali Friendship Association for Peace and Development officially formed in Toronto.
Fall
    EMM sends two missionary nurses to Mogadishu.

1993
June
    Because of heavy fighting in Mogadishu, EMM missionary nurses evacuated.
August
    MCC gives financial support to a five-month convening of Somali clan elders working to resolve conflicts.

1994
    Among many deaths, three believers assassinated.

1996
November
    Representative for EMM and MCC Somali/Somaliland visits Mogadishu, Johar, and Mahaddei.

1997-8
    MCC funds several women's peace conferences.

2000
February
    EMM assigns a couple to teach spring semester at Amoud University in Somaliland.
October
    Transitional National Government tries to reunite Somalia. Lacking popular support, it fails even to reunite Mogadishu.

2002
January
    MCC funds Mogadishu workshop on AIDS problems.

2003
    Joint EMM and MCC efforts continue with Somalis in peacemaking, education, fellowship, development, and relief.

Mennonite workers in Somalia

NAME	ADDRESS IN 2002	POSITION/ORGANIZATION	YEARS	COUNTRY
Ali, Helen Landis	Lancaster, PA	Registered Nurse, EMM	1956-63	Somalia
Beachy, Alice-Ann	Washington, DC	Intern, EMM	1996-98	Djibouti
Beachy, Bertha M.	Goshen, IN	Teacher/Bookstore, EMM	1958-76	Somalia
		Literacy Worker, EMM	1976-78	Kenya
		Mission Representative, EMM/MCC	1995-2000	Kenya
Becker, Esther M.	Lititz, PA	Teacher, EMM	1975-76	Somalia
Bergey, Bonnie S.	Lancaster, PA	Teacher, EMM	1990-93	Somalia
		Mission Representative, EMM/MCC	1993-95	Kenya
Biber, Douglas	Unknown	Literacy Worker, EMM	1978-80	Kenya
Biber, Teresa	Unknown	Literacy Worker, EMM	1978-80	Kenya
Bradshaw, Bruce B.	North Newton, KS	Teacher, EMM	1985-87	Somalia
Bradshaw, Mary F.	North Newton, KS	Hospital Volunteer, EMM	1985-87	Somalia
Brislen, Cynthia	Djiboutiville, Djibouti	Nurse/Mission Director, EMM	1990-present	Djibouti
Brislen, Michael	Djiboutiville, Djibouti	Teacher, EMM	1990-present	Djibouti
Brower, Adri	Netherlands	Teacher, EMM	1988-89	Somalia
Brown, Lena Horning	Grantham, PA	Teacher, EMM	1962-66	Somalia
Brubaker, Erma R.	Mount Joy, PA	Homemaker, EMM	1966-71	Somalia
Brubaker, J. Allen	Mount Joy, PA	Agricultural Worker, EMM	1957-60	Somalia
		Teacher, EMM	1966-71	Somalia
Brubaker, J. Dean	Lancaster, PA	Teacher, EMM	1983-86	Kenya
Brubaker, Nancy	Lancaster, PA	Teacher, EMM	1983-86	Kenya
Brubaker, A. Hope	Mifflintown, PA	Registered Nurse, EMM	1967-75	Somalia
		Islamic Ministries Worker, EMM	1977-82	Kenya
Brubaker, Roy L.	Mifflintown, PA	Teacher, EMM	1967-75	Somalia
		Islamic Ministries Worker, EMM	1977-82	Kenya
Buckwalter, Betty Lou	Fulks Run, VA	Homemaker, EMM	1972-73	Somalia
Buckwalter, Robert	Fulks Run, VA	Agricultural, EMM	1972-73	Somalia
Coverdale, Scott	Tucson, AZ	Community Services, MCC	1984-87	Somalia
Cressman, Elsie	Kitchener, ON, Can.	Midwife, EMM	1971	Somalia
Dannelly, Jay	Deceased	Teacher, MCC	1979-89	Kenya
Dannelly, Sylvia	Pecos, TX	Teacher, MCC	1979-89	Kenya
Derksen, John	Winnipeg, MB, Can.	Logistics worker, EMM	1993	Somalia

NAME	ADDRESS IN 2002	POSITION/ORGANIZATION	YEARS	COUNTRY
Dorsch, Victor	New Hamburg, ON, Can.	Administrator, EMM	1956-70	Somalia
Dorsch, Viola	New Hamburg, ON, Can.	Homemaker/Teacher, EMM	1956-70	Somalia
Dunk, Bruce	Paris, ON, Can.	Agricultural Extension, MCC	1985-88	Somalia
Dunk, Catherine	Paris, ON, Can.	Agricultural Extension, MCC	1985-88	Somalia
Eby, Omar E.	Harrisonburg, VA	Teacher, EMM	1957-60	Somalia
Elzinga, Nancy	Lambertville, MI	Educator, MCC	1974-77	Kenya
Elzinga, Steve	Lambertville, MI	Ag/Food Securities worker, MCC	1974-77	Kenya
Fast, Deb *(spouse: M. Wiebe)*	Amman, Jordan	Adult Educator, MCC	1991-94	Kenya
Frey, Ardith	Winnipeg, MB, Can.	Country Representative, MCC	1981-84	Somalia
Frey, Marvin	Winnipeg, MB, Can.	Country Representative, MCC	1981-84	Somalia
Gehman, Mary W.	Reinholds, PA	Teacher, EMM	1958-76, 1983-87, 1990	Somalia
Gerber, Daniel K.	Lombard, IL	Health Ministry worker, EMM	1987-88	Somalia
Gerber, Jan E.	Lombard, IL	Health Ministry worker, EMM	1987-88	Somalia
Gilrein, Daniel	Riverhead, NY	Horticulturist, MCC	1983-86	Somalia
Good, Elaine R.	Lititz, PA	Community Development worker, EMM	1969-72	Somalia
		Teacher, EMM	2000	Somaliland
Good, Leon W.	Lititz, PA	Community Development worker, EMM	1969-72	Somalia
		Teacher, EMM	2000	Somaliland
Gorvett, Lou Murray	Kitchener, ON, Can.	Community Service/Country Representative, MCC	1981-85	Somalia
Gray, Albert L.	Berea, OH	Teacher, EMM	1982-84	Somalia
Gray, Louise N.	Berea, OH	Teacher, EMM	1982-84	Somalia
Grill, Frances	Elkhart, IN	Public Health worker, MCC	1983-88	Kenya
Grill, Peter	Elkhart, IN	Animal Husbandry worker, MCC	1983-88	Kenya
Groff, Paul E.	Harrisonburg, VA	Administrative Assistant, MCC	1993-97	Kenya
Grove, Dorothy H.	Cambridge, ON, Can.	Registered Nurse, EMM	1960-62, 1985	Somalia
Grove, Merlin R.	Deceased	Teacher/Administrator, EMM	1960-62	Somalia
Harder, James	Bluffton, OH	Secondary Education worker, MCC	1981-84	Kenya
Harder, Karen	Bluffton, OH	Dietician, MCC	1981-84	Kenya
Hartzler, Ronald L.	Newton, KS	Teacher, EMM	1971-73	Somalia
		Eastleigh Centre Worker, EMM	1973-74	Kenya
Hartzler, Ruth Ann	Newton, KS	Teacher, EMM	1971-73	Somalia
		Eastleigh Centre Worker, EMM	1973-74	Kenya

NAME	ADDRESS IN 2002	POSITION/ORGANIZATION	YEARS	COUNTRY
Heistand, Gerald M.	Elizabethtown, PA	Agricultural Engineer, MCC	1980-83	Somalia
Hicks, Lois Ranck	Elizabethtown, PA	Intern, EMM	1983-84	Kenya
		Nurse, EMM	1984-86	Kenya
Hinton, Audrey	St. Paul, MN	Islamic Ministries worker, EMM	1988-92	Kenya
Hinton, Mark	St. Paul, MN	Islamic Ministries worker, EMM	1988-92	Kenya
Histand, Lowell	Doylestown, PA	Business Administrator, MCC	1974	Kenya
Hooley, Jane Myers	Leola, PA	Teacher, EMM	1971-76	Somalia
Horst, Martha E.	Dalton, OH	Registered Nurse, EMM	1969-73	Somalia
Hostetler, Marian E.	Elkhart, IN	Teacher, EMM	1988-89	Somalia
		Teacher, EMM	1990-93	Djibouti
Housman, Harold	Lititz, PA	Doctor, EMM	1965	Somalia
Housman, Miriam	Lititz, PA	Homemaker, EMM	1965	Somalia
Jantzi, Terry	Harrisonburg, VA	Refugee Assistance worker, MCC	1989	Somalia
Kauffman, Christine *(spouse: T. Shenk)*	Lancaster, PA	Refugee Worker, EMM	1993-94	Kenya
Keener, Clayton	Deceased	Administrator, EMM	1957-58	Somalia
Keener, Martha	Deceased	Teacher, EMM	1957-58	Somalia
Kehler, Dennis	Toronto, ON, Can.	Community Services worker, MCC	1983-86	Somalia
Kehler, Esther W.	Toronto, ON, Can.	Public Health, MCC	1983-86	Somalia
Kennel, Rhoda C.	Mountville, PA	Teacher, EMM	1969-73	Somalia
King, Esther Mack	Pottstown, PA	Registered Nurse, EMM	1967-73	Somalia
Kniss, Fred	Chicago, IL	Islamic Ministries worker, EMM	1979-84	Kenya
Kniss, Rosalyn	Chicago, IL	Eastleigh Centre worker, EMM	1979-84	Kenya
Kratz, Elizabeth H.	Sellersville, PA	Homemaker, EMM	1969-71	Somalia
Kratz, Vernon H.	Sellersville, PA	Doctor, EMM	1969-71	Somalia
Kurtz, Catherine E.	Lancaster, PA	Homemaker, EMM	1962-74	Somalia
Kurtz, Chester I.	Lancaster, PA	Agricultural Worker, EMM	1955-59	Somalia
		Teacher, EMM	1962-74	Somalia
Lamman, Anne M.	La Junta, CO	Community Services worker, MCC	1987-89	Somalia
Lamman, John S.	La Junta, CO	Agriculture/Food Securities worker, MCC	1988-89	Somalia
Larimer, Dean B.	Bakersfield, CA	Teacher, EMM	1990-93	Djibouti
Larimer, Sandy L.	Bakersfield, CA	Teacher, EMM	1990-93	Djibouti
Laroche, David Adoph *(spouse: B.J. Linquist)*	Marsabit, Kenya	Animal Husbandry worker, MCC	1988-92	Kenya
Leaman, Ivan B.	Strasburg, PA	Doctor, EMM	1960-69, 1990	Somalia
Leaman, Mary Ellen	Strasburg, PA	Homemaker, EMM	1960-69, 1990	Somalia
Leaman, M. Hershey	Landisville, PA	Hospital administrator, EMM	1960-61	Somalia
Leaman, Norma H.	Landisville, PA	Homemaker, EMM	1960-61	Somalia

NAME	ADDRESS IN 2002	POSITION/ORGANIZATION	YEARS	COUNTRY
Lehman, Anna Lutz	Lititz, PA	Registered Nurse, EMM	1960-73	Somalia
Lehman, Cora E.	Chambersburg, PA	Registered Nurse, EMM	1976	Somalia
Lehman, Helen Ranck	Deceased	Teacher, EMM	1961-76	Somalia
Lehman, Janel E.	Djiboutiville, Djibouti	School Nurse, EMM	2001-present	Djibouti
Lind, Rhoda H.	Lititz, PA	Homemaker/Teacher, EMM	1953-67	Somalia
Lind, Wilbert G.	Lititz, PA	Administrator, EMM	1953-67	Somalia
Linquist, B.J. *(spouse: D. A. Laroche)*	Marsabit, Kenya	Animal Husbandry worker, MCC	1988-92	Kenya
Litwiller, Kenneth	Lewistown, PA	Agricultural Engineer, MCC	1978-81	Kenya
Litwiller, Laura	Lewistown, PA	Horticulturist, MCC	1978-81	Kenya
Loewen, E. Ronald	Deceased	Doctor, EMM/MCC	1972	Somalia
Loewen, Viola H.	Kenora, ON, Can.	Homemaker, EMM/MCC	1972	Somalia
Logan, Chantal S.	Nairobi, Kenya	French Teacher, EMM	1995-99	Djibouti
		Co-mission director, EMM/MCC	2000-present	Kenya
Logan, Mark A.	Nairobi, Kenya	Mission Director, EMM	1995-99	Djibouti
		Co-mission director, EMM/MCC	2000-present	Kenya
Longenecker, Rebecca H.	Elizabethtown, PA	Registered Nurse, EMM	1967	Somalia
Luper, Deborah	Anchorage, AK	Appropriate Technologies worker, MCC	1987-89	Somalia
Lutz, Martha Jane	Deceased	Teacher, EMM	1965-68	Somalia
Martin, Raymond S.	McLean, VA	Agricultural worker, EMM	1961-63	Somalia
Martin, Susan P.	Gap, PA	Registered Nurse, EMM	1990	Somalia
Martin, Thomas K.	Gap, PA	Registered Nurse, EMM	1990	Somalia
Mauk, Hollie	Williamsport, PA	Community worker, MCC	1984-87	Somalia
McGinnis, Thad	Henderson, KY	Water Resources worker, MCC	1979-82	Somalia
Merryman, James	Bear Creek, PA	Teacher, MCC	1971-74	Kenya
Merryman, Nancy	Bear Creek, PA	Teacher, MCC	1972-74	Kenya
Metzler, Marilyn J.	Richmond, VA	Registered Nurse, EMM	1993-94	Somalia
		Registered Nurse, EMM	1994-95	Djibouti
Miller, Daniel E.	Unknown	Teacher, EMM/MCC	1971	Somalia
Miller, Marlene K.	Unknown	Teacher, EMM/MCC	1971	Somalia
Miller, Fae	Orrville, OH	Registered Nurse, EMM	1953-71	Somalia
		Teacher, EMM	1981-83	Somalia
Miller, Gerald K.	Uniondale, IN	Doctor, EMM	1971-72	Somalia
Miller, Mary M.	Uniondale, IN	Homemaker, EMM	1971-72	Somalia
Miller, V. David	Deceased	Builder, EMM	1958-61	Somalia
Minor, Erika M.	Djiboutiville, Djibouti	Community Service worker, EMM	1993-94, 1997-present	Djibouti
Minor, Sean E.	Djiboutiville, Djibouti	English Teacher, EMM	1997-present	Djibouti

NAME	ADDRESS IN 2002	POSITION/ORGANIZATION	YEARS	COUNTRY
Morrow, Dorcas Stoltzfus	Blue Bell, PA	Doctor, EMM	1963-64	Somalia
Mumaw, Catherine R.	Corvallis, OR	Non-formal Educator, MCC	1981-82	Somalia
Mummert, Mark	Unknown	Intern, EMM	1983-84	Kenya
Mummert, Mary	Unknown	Intern, EMM	1983-84	Kenya
Musser, Marvin S.	Goshen, IN	Agricultural worker, EMM	1955-59	Somalia
Myer, Everett	Cranberry Twp., PA	Teacher, EMM	1969-72	Somalia
Myer, Leona S.	Cranberry Twp., PA	Registered Nurse, EMM	1969-72	Somalia
Nafziger, Kenneth L.	State College, PA	Teacher, EMM	1983-86	Kenya
Nafziger, Judy	State College, PA	Physical Therapy Nurse, EMM	1985-86	Kenya
Newswanger, Marian E.	Deceased	Community Development worker, EMM	1990	Somalia
Newswanger, Wesley	Lancaster, PA	Community Development worker, EMM	1990	Somalia
Nissley, Elizabeth G.	Mount Joy, PA	Registered Nurse, EMM	1966-73, 1983-86	Somalia
Nissley, Kenneth M.	Mount Joy, PA	Administrator/Teacher, EMM	1966-73	Somalia
		Teacher, EMM	1983-86	Somalia
Nzesi, Velma Eshleman	Deceased	Registered Nurse, EMM	1971-73	Somalia
		Registered Nurse, EMM	1973-74	Kenya
Plank, Caroline	Harrisonburg, VA	Teacher, EMM	1952-53	Somalia
Rands, Barry	Ventura, CA	Agricultural Engineer, MCC	1980-83	Somalia
Rands, Janine	Ventura, CA	Community Services worker, MCC	1980-83	Somalia
Reimer, Cornelius E. (Neil)	Chilliwack, BC, Can.	Business Manager, EMM/MCC	1971-76	Somalia
		Teacher, EMM/MCC	1981-83	Somalia
Reimer, Margaret I.	Chilliwack, BC, Can.	Teacher, EMM/MCC	1971-76, 1981-83	Somalia
Reed, Barbara K.	Lancaster, PA	Registered Nurse, EMM	1961-74	Somalia
Reed, Harold E.	Lancaster, PA	Administrator/Teacher, EMM	1961-74	Somalia
Rempel, Henry J.	Winnipeg, MB, Can.	Agricultural Extension worker, MCC	1980-83	Somalia
Rissler, G. Edward	Harrisonburg, VA	Teacher, EMM	1972-76, 1985-87	Somalia
		Teacher, EMM	1976-79	Kenya
Rissler, Jean E.	Harrisonburg, VA	Teacher, EMM	1972-76, 1985-87	Somalia
		Teacher, EMM	1976-79	Kenya
Roth, Annabelle	Lancaster, PA	Homemaker, EMM	1972-74	Somalia
Roth, Glen A.	Lancaster, PA	Teacher, EMM	1972-74	Somalia
Rudy, Carolyn	Quezon City, Philippines	Community Services worker, MCC	1987-89	Somalia
Rudy, Jonathan	Quezon City, Philippines	Community Services worker, MCC	1987-89	Somalia
Salim, Rhoda Buckwalter	Willow Street, PA	Registered Nurse, EMM	1964-66	Somalia
Samatar, Lydia Glick	South Orange, NJ	Teacher, EMM	1963-71	Somalia
Schaupp, Cindi	Nairobi, Kenya	Teacher, EMM	1997-present	Kenya

NAME	ADDRESS IN 2002	POSITION/ORGANIZATION	YEARS	COUNTRY
Schaupp, Darren	Nairobi, Kenya	Islamic Ministries worker, EMM	1997-present	Kenya
Segerstrom, Miriam Leaman	Tucson, AZ	Registered Nurse, EMM	1961-70	Somalia
Sensenig, J. Carl	Denver, PA	Teacher, EMM	1986-89	Somalia
Sensenig, Julie A.	Denver, PA	Registered Nurse, EMM	1986-89	Somalia
Shelly, Gloria J.	Deceased	Homemaker, EMM	1965-70	Somalia
Shelly, James C.	Meridian, ID	Business Manager, EMM	1965-70	Somalia
Shenk, David W.	Mountville, PA	Teacher, EMM	1963-73	Somalia
		Teacher, Islamic ministries, EMM	1973-79	Kenya
Shenk, Grace	Mountville, PA	Homemaker, EMM	1963-73	Somalia
		Homemaker, EMM	1973-79	Kenya
Shenk, Douglas L.	Middletown, PA	Teacher, EMM	1992-96	Djibouti
Shenk, Elaine C.	Middletown, PA	Teacher, EMM	1992-96	Djibouti
Shenk, Timothy (spouse: C. Kauffman)	Lancaster, PA	Refugee worker, EMM	1993-94	Kenya
Shires, Julie Janzen	Arroyo Grande, CA	Country Representative, MCC	1988-89	Somalia
Shirk, Edna E.	Myerstown, PA	Homemaker, EMM	1955-59	Somalia
Shirk, Leroy F.	Myerstown, PA	Builder, EMM	1955-59	Somalia
Short, Michael	Archbold, OH	Mechanic, MCC	1982-84	Somalia
Short, Peggy	Archbold, OH	Public Health, MCC	1982-84	Somalia
Smoker, Naomi	Chesterfield, MO	Secretary/Bookkeeper, EMM	1967-74	Somalia
		Office Assistant, EMM	1974-77	Kenya
Sommers, Eloise	Lakewood, CO	Country Representative, MCC	1985-88	Somalia
Sommers, Myron	Lakewood, CO	Country Representative, MCC	1985-88	Somalia
Spencer, Jay	Bloomingdale, IL	Intern, EMM	1990	Kenya
Stauffer, Constance F.	Lancaster, PA	Teacher, EMM	1961-65	Somalia
Stauffer, Harold S.	Lancaster, PA	Administrator, EMM	1961-65	Somalia
Stoehr, Annette	Ann Arbor, MI	Administrative Assistant, MCC	1997-2001	Kenya
Stoltzfus, Daniel	Sarasota, FL	Agricultural worker, EMM	1959-62	Somalia
Stutzman, E. Yvonne	Harrisonburg, VA	Eastleigh Centre worker, EMM	1989-92	Kenya
Stutzman, Marvin	Harrisonburg, VA	Eastleigh Centre worker, EMM	1989-92	Kenya
Thuma, Barb	Fort Wayne, IN	Agronomy worker, MCC	1982-85	Somalia
Tung, Ann Drustrude	Portland, OR	Dietician/Nutrition worker, MCC	1985-88	Somalia
Unruh, Selma	North Newton, KS	Agricultural Administrator, MCC	1980	Somalia
Unruh, Willard	Deceased	Agricultural Administration, MCC	1980	Somalia
Van Pelt, Elsie	Columbiana, OH	Teacher, EMM	1964-74	Somalia
Weaver, Naomi	Kirkwood, PA	Registered Nurse, EMM	1998	Somalia

NAME	ADDRESS IN 2002	POSITION/ORGANIZATION	YEARS	COUNTRY
Weaver, Verda	Goshen, IN	Registered Nurse, EMM	1993-96	Somalia
		Registered Nurse, EMM	1998	Kenya
Weinman, David	Tucson, AZ	Religious/Theological educator, MCC	1980-85	Kenya
Weinman, Joyce	Tucson, AZ	Educator/Community worker, MCC	1980-85	Kenya
Wenger, Rhoda E.	Lititz, PA	Teacher, EMM	1971-76	Somalia
Wert, Daniel	Lancaster, PA	Registered Nurse, EMM	1965	Somalia
Wesselhoeft, Carl J.	Logan, OH	Teacher, EMM	1955-66	Somalia
Wesselhoeft, Leota F.	Logan, OH	Homemaker, EMM	1955-66	Somalia
Wiebe, Menno (spouse: Deb Fast)	Amman, Jordan	Justice Researcher, MCC	1991-94	Kenya
Witmer, Barbara S.	Lancaster, PA	Agricultural worker, EMM	1986-88	Somalia
		Agricultural worker, EMM	1991-92	Kenya
Witmer, R. Lamar	Lancaster, PA	Agricultural educator, EMM	1986-88	Somalia
		Agricultural worker, EMM	1991-92	Kenya
Yoder, Don	Harrisonburg, VA	Eastleigh Centre worker, EMM	1985-89	Kenya
Yoder, Em	Harrisonburg, VA	Eastleigh Centre worker, EMM	1985-89	Kenya
Yoder, Kevin L.	Nairobi, Kenya	Teacher, EMM	1986-90	Somalia
Yoder, Sharon E.	Nairobi, Kenya	Teacher, EMM	1986-90	Somalia
Yost, Ivan R.	Christiana, PA	Agricultural worker, EMM	1959-61	Somalia
Zimmerman, Jeffrey	Mount Joy, PA	Intern, EMM	1983-84	Kenya
Zimmerman, Pauline	Lancaster, PA	Registered Nurse, EMM	1970-73	Somalia
		Registered Nurse, EMM	1974-76	Kenya
Zook, John E.	Leola, PA	Builder, EMM	1969-73	Somalia
Zook, Velma J.	Leola, PA	Homemaker, EMM	1969-73	Somalia

Maps

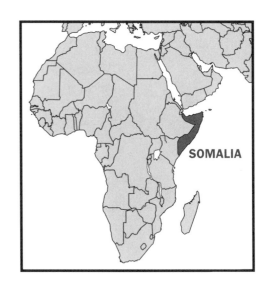

*Spellings vary for place names within Somalia.

Healing River

O healing river, send down your waters,
Send down your waters upon this land.
O healing river, send down your waters,
And wash the blood from off the sand.

This land is parching, this land is burning,
No seed is growing in the barren ground.
O healing river, send down your waters,
O healing river, send your waters down.

Let the seed of freedom awake and flourish,
Let the deep roots nourish, let the tall stalks rise.
O healing river, send down your waters,
O healing river, from out of the skies.

Text: anonymous
Music: traditional hymn melody

About the author

Omar Eby taught in the Somalia Mennonite Mission English night school for adults, Mogadiscio, 1957-1960. He edited Eastern Mennonite Missions' *Missionary Messenger* from 1962-1966 (Salunga, Pa.), and was Director of Information Services, Mennonite Central Committee (Akron, Pa.), 1967-1970. Taking graduate degrees from Syracuse University and the University of Virginia, he taught English literature and writing at Eastern Mennonite University (Harrisonburg, Va.) for 27 years. He began early retirement in 1999 to pursue writing full time. Omar lives with his wife, Anna Kathryn (Shenk) Eby in Harrisonburg; they are the parents of three children and the grandparents of three granddaughters.

Omar Eby, the author, in Mogadiscio where he taught English, 1959.